Colorado's *Authentic* Coloring Book for Stoners

Volume One
by
Ruth Mason

Copyright December 2015
All rights reserved

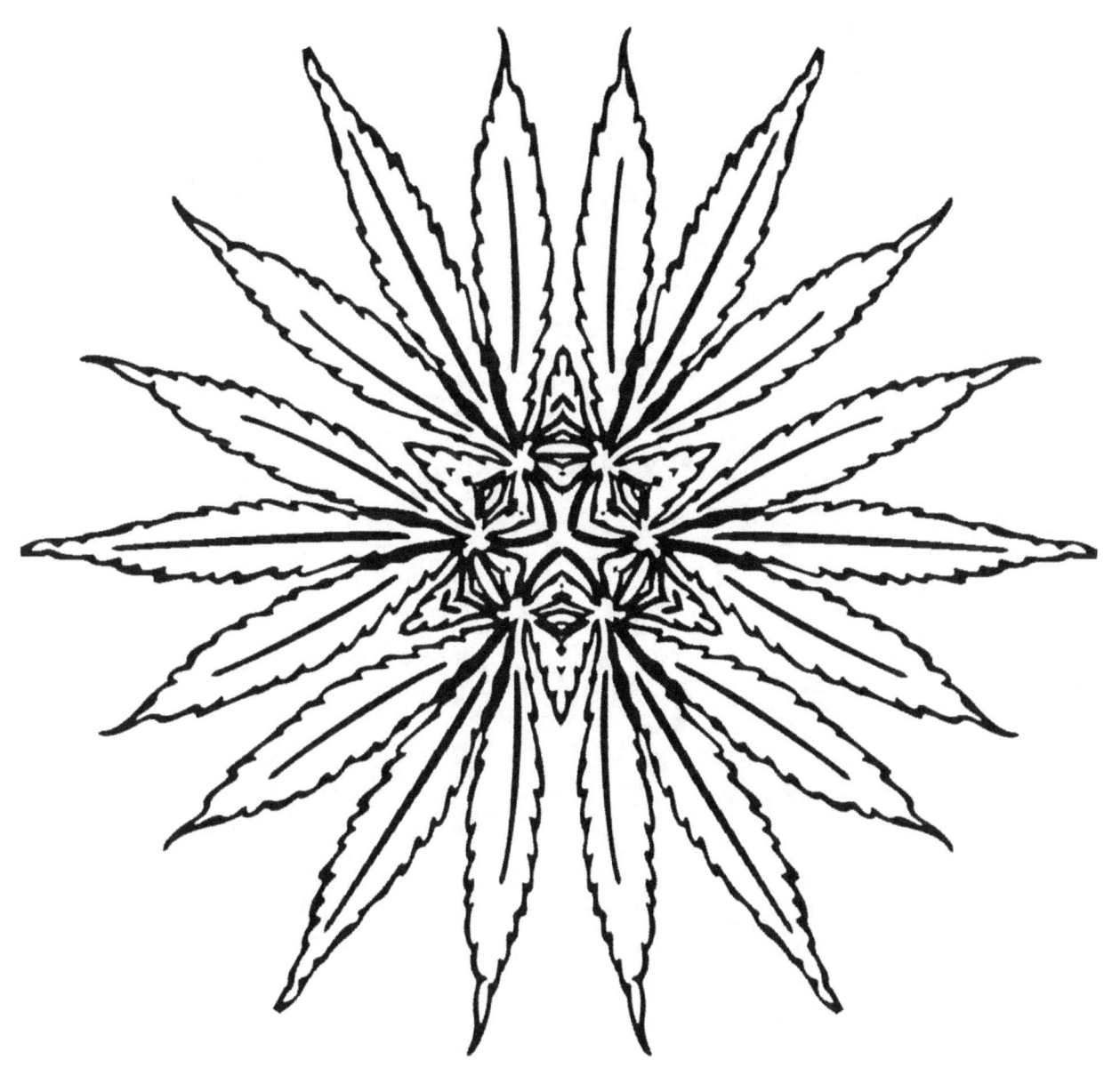

There are many mediums you can use to color. I suggest using markers, colored pencils, gel pens, or watercolor pencils.

You might want to put a blank piece of paper or thin cardboard behind the design before you begin to color. This will catch any bleed through.

If you like, please join my FaceBook page, Coloring Designs, where you can post comments and your beautiful artwork.

Enjoy!

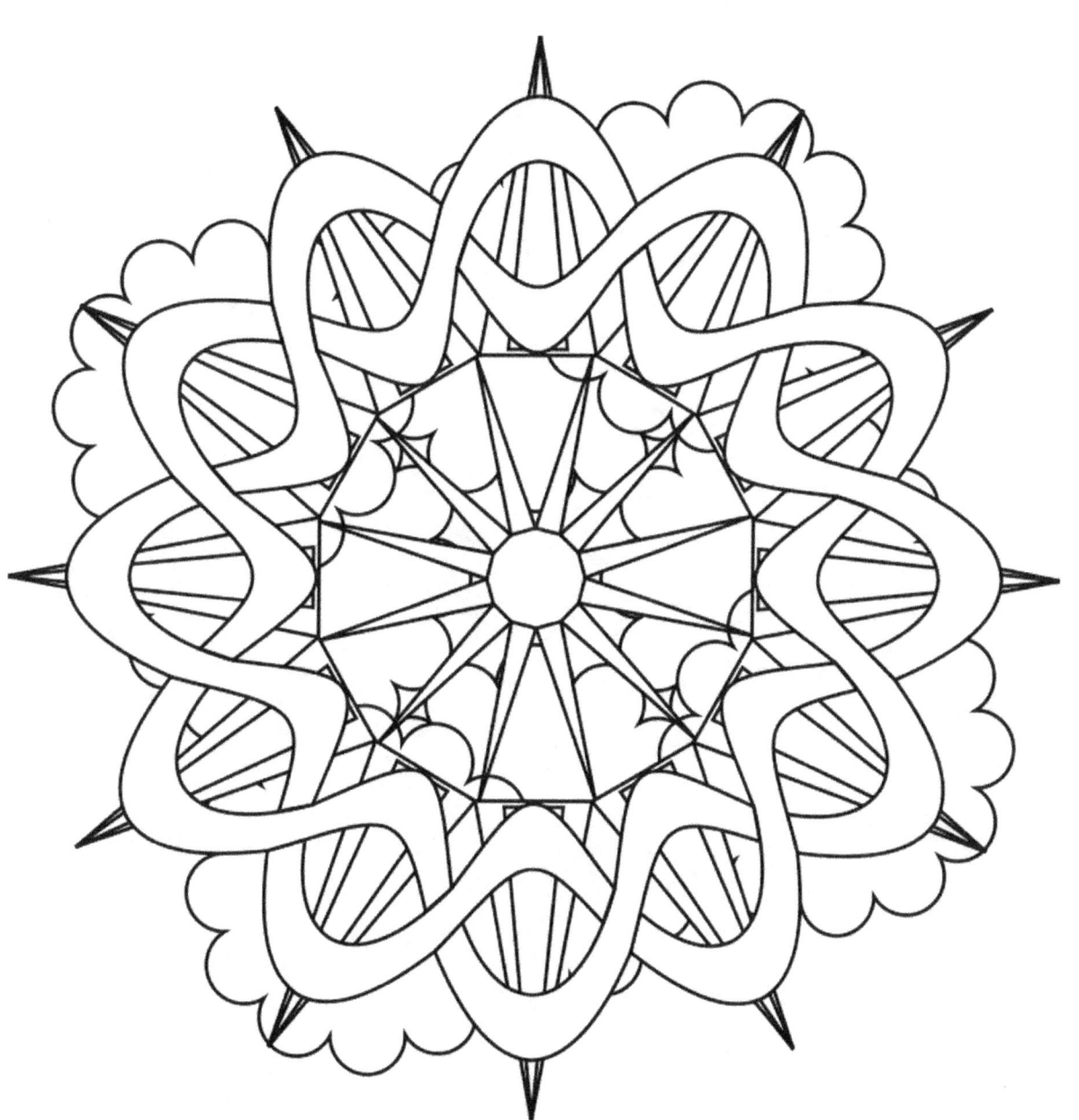

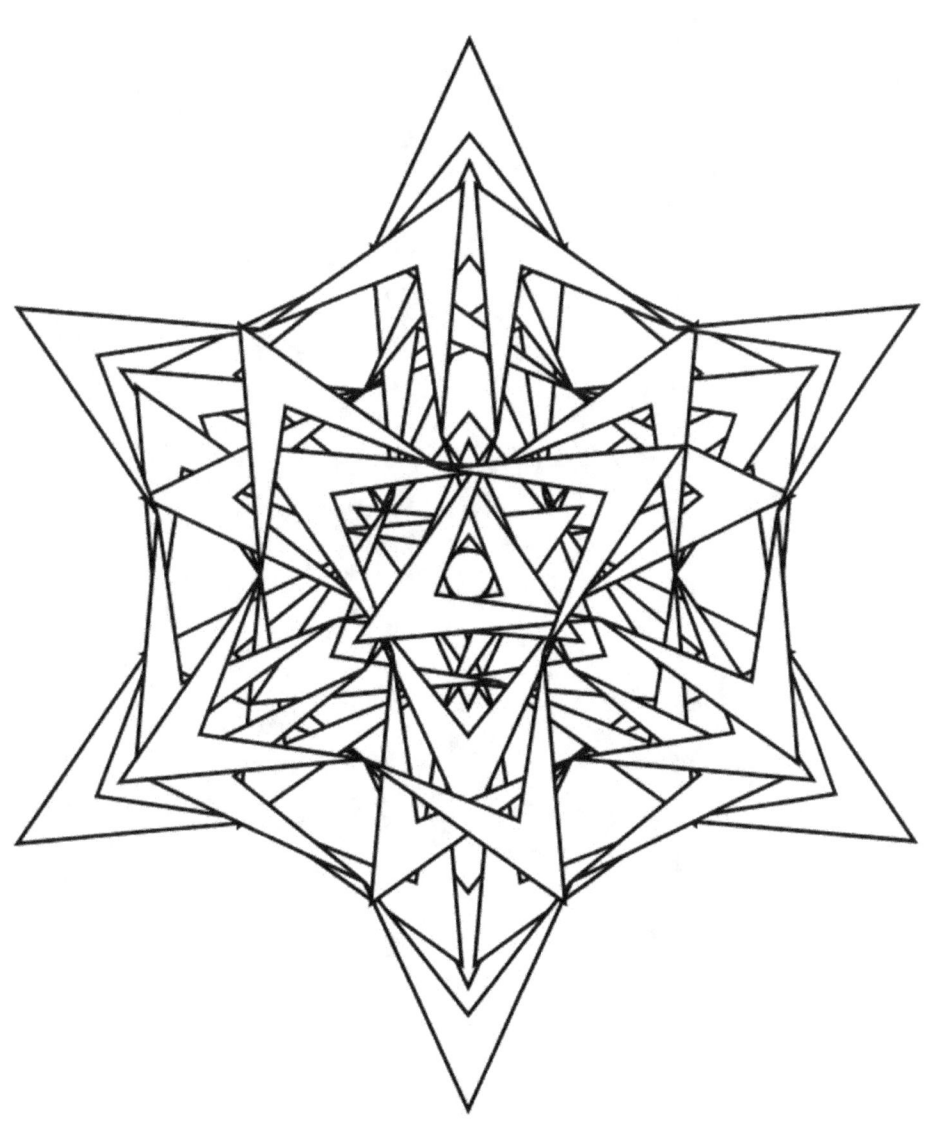

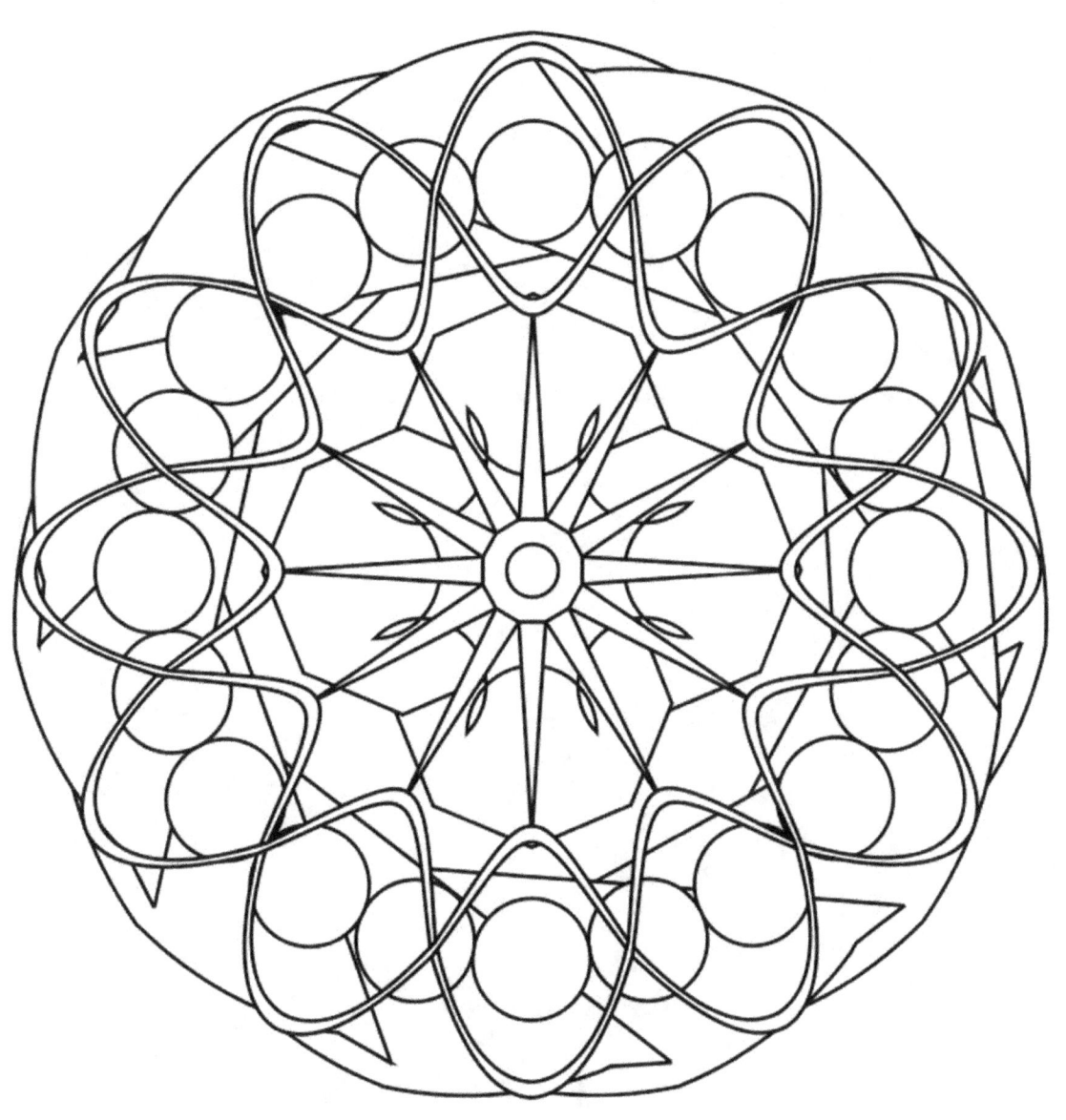

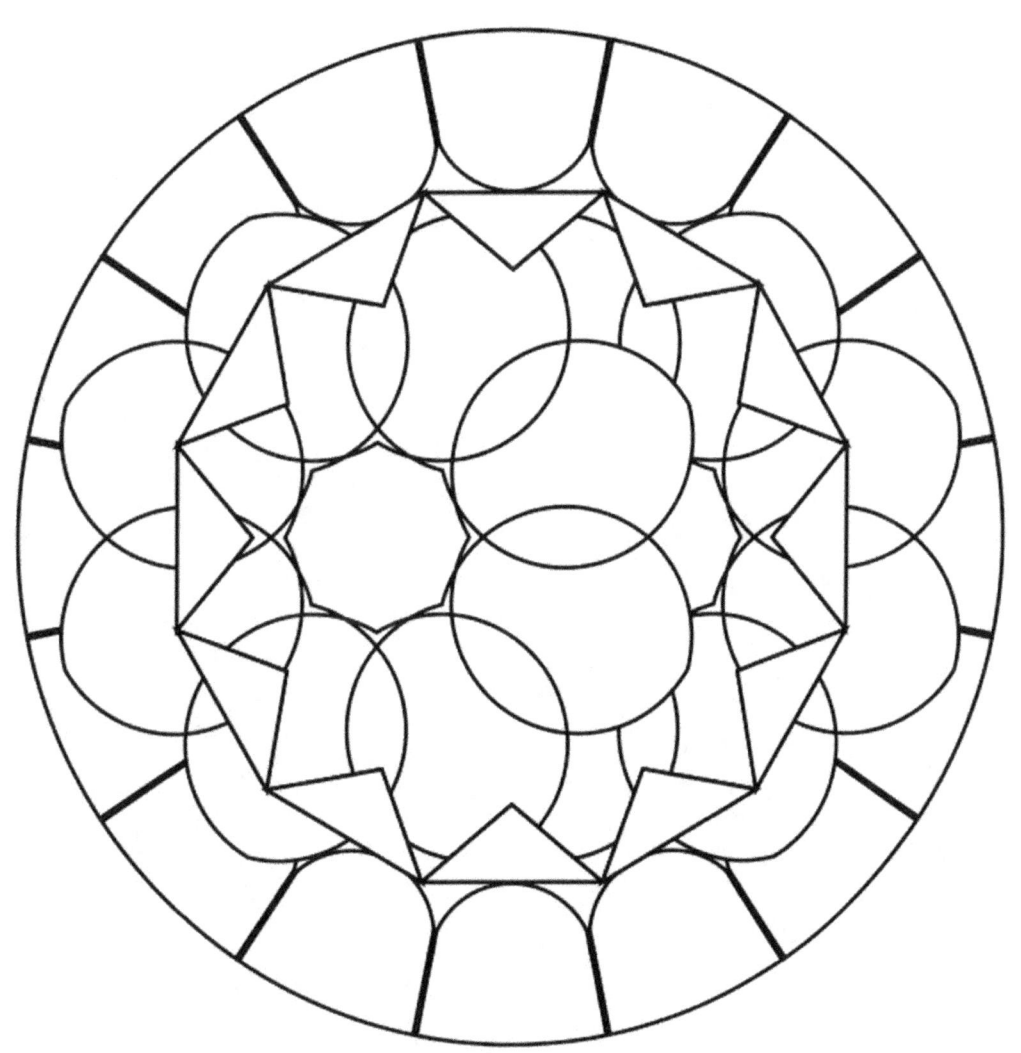

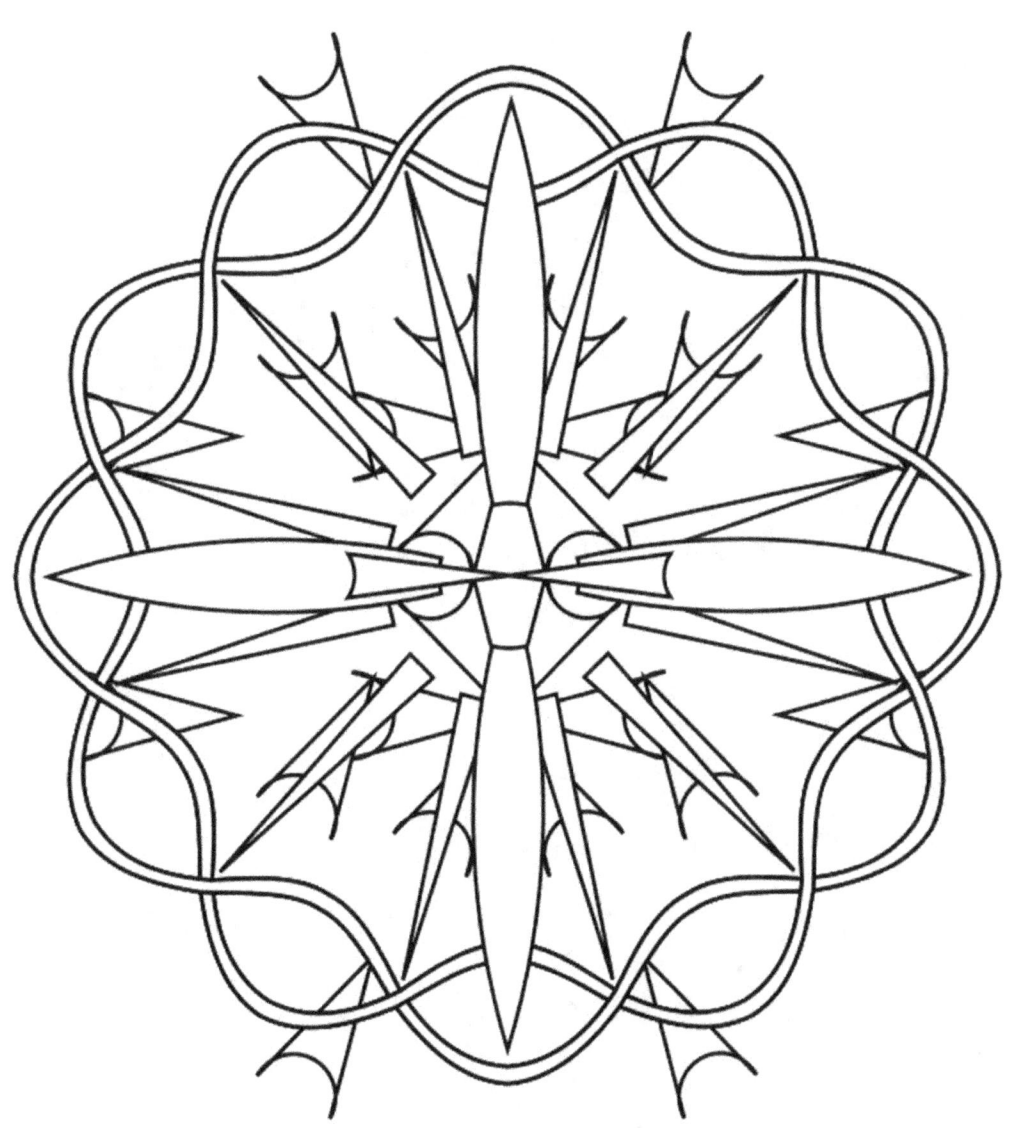

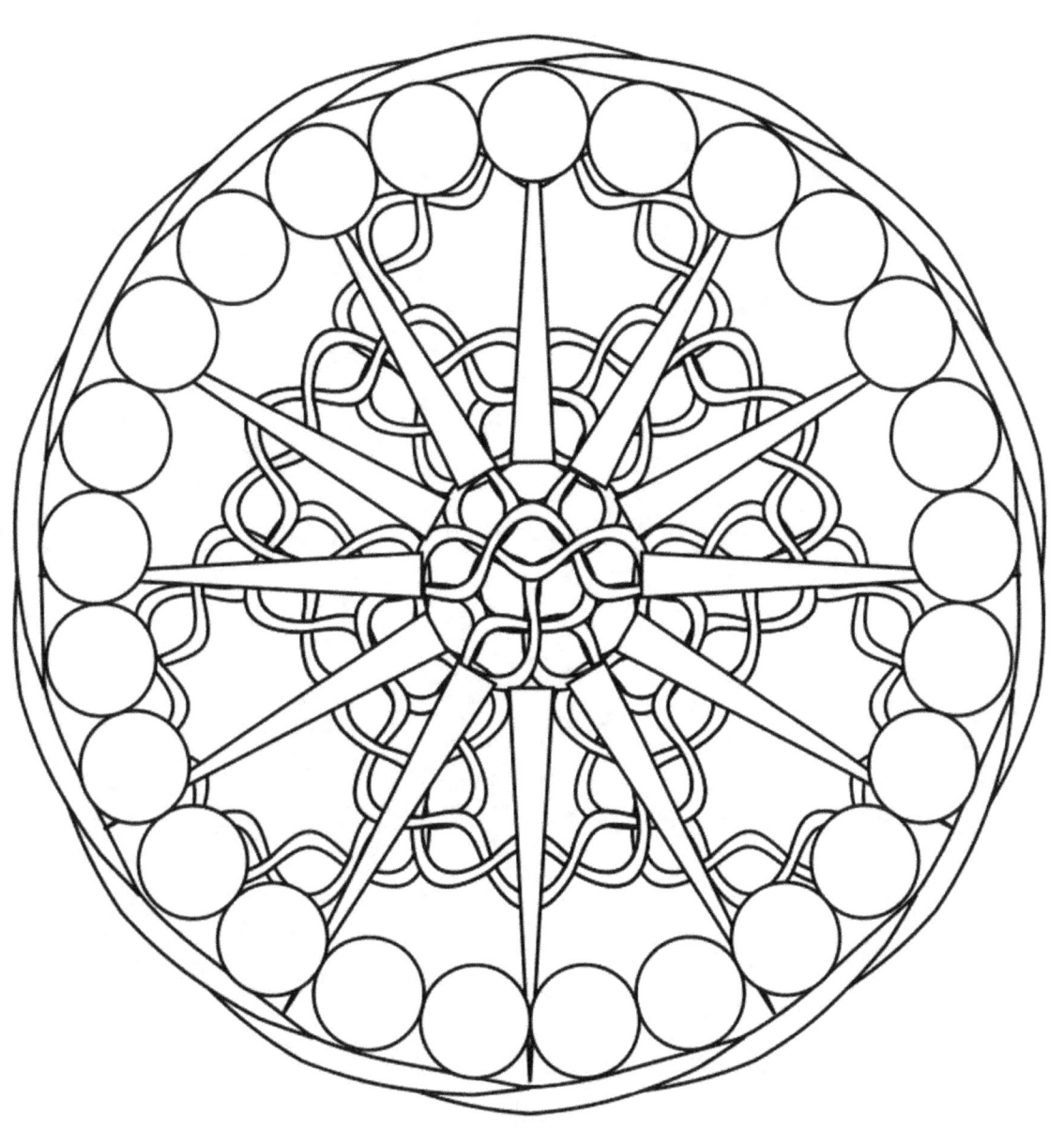

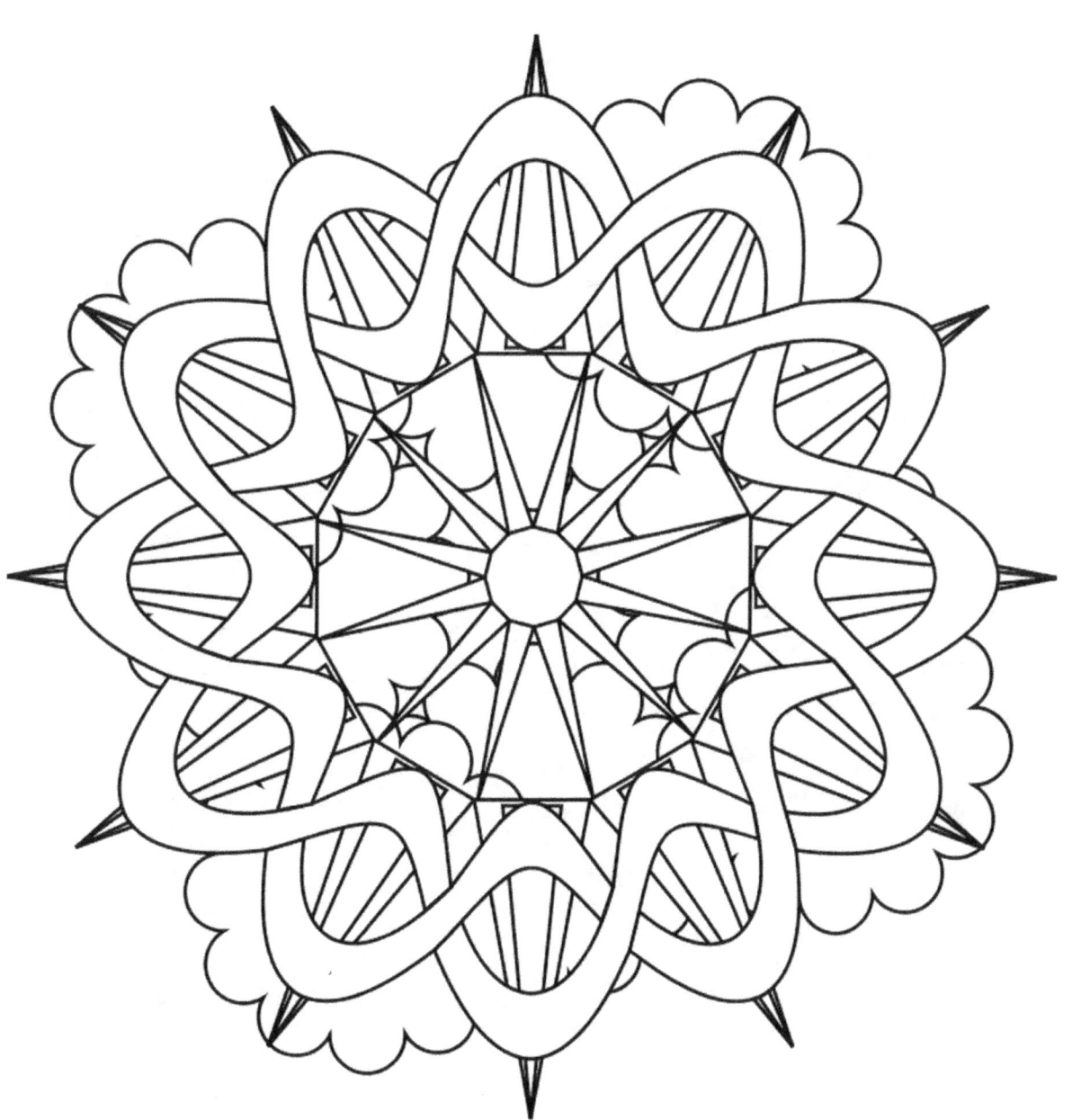

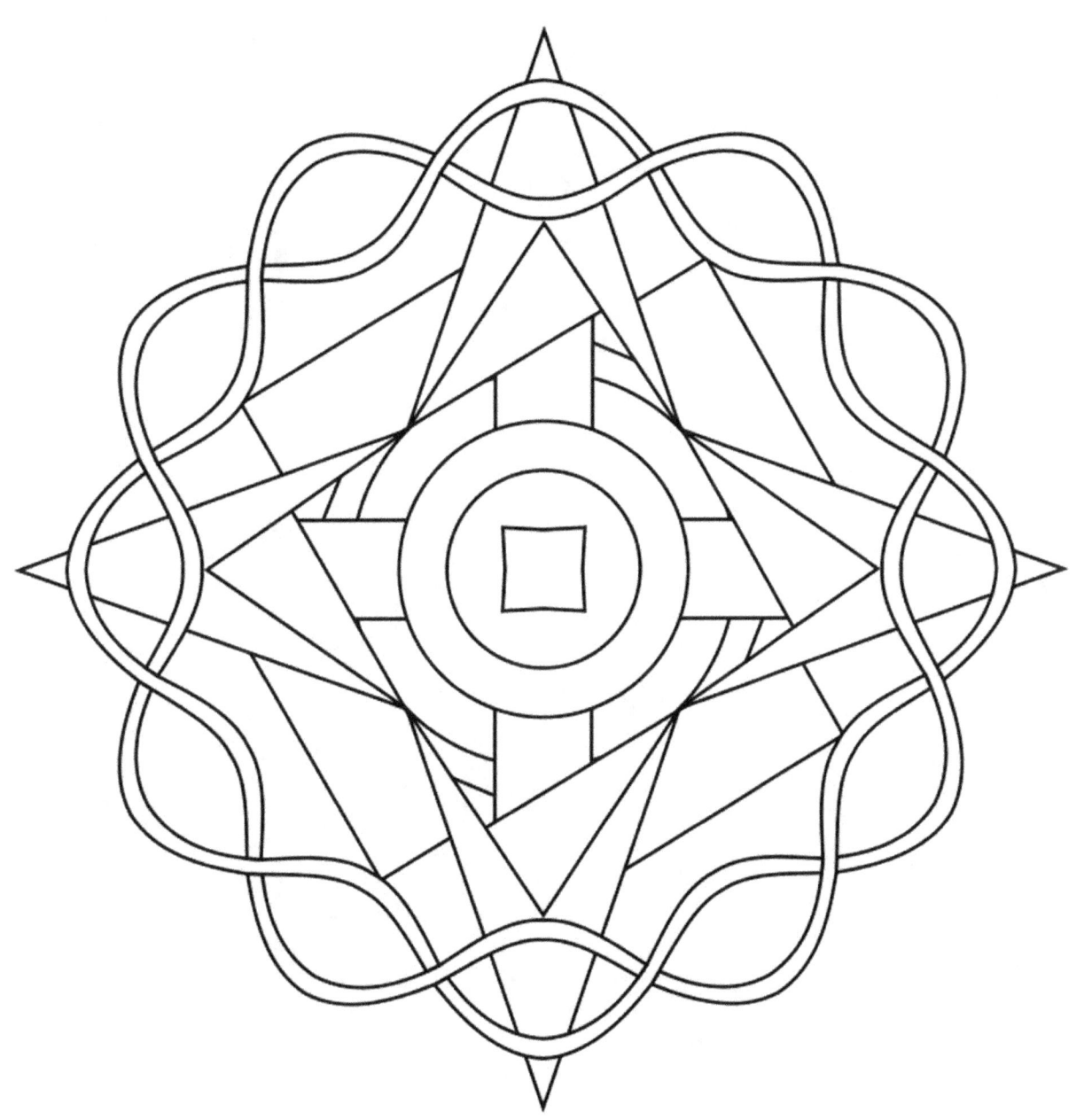

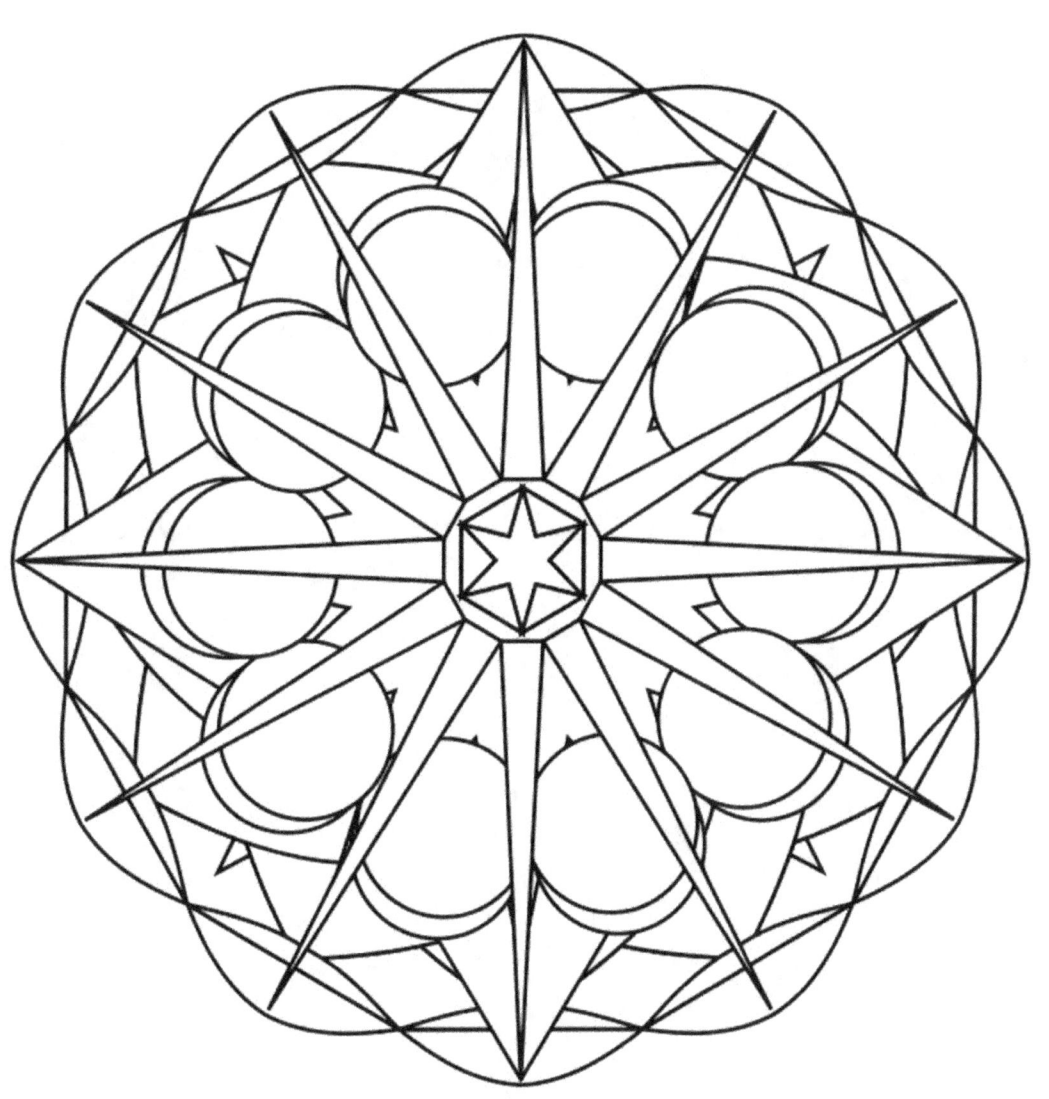

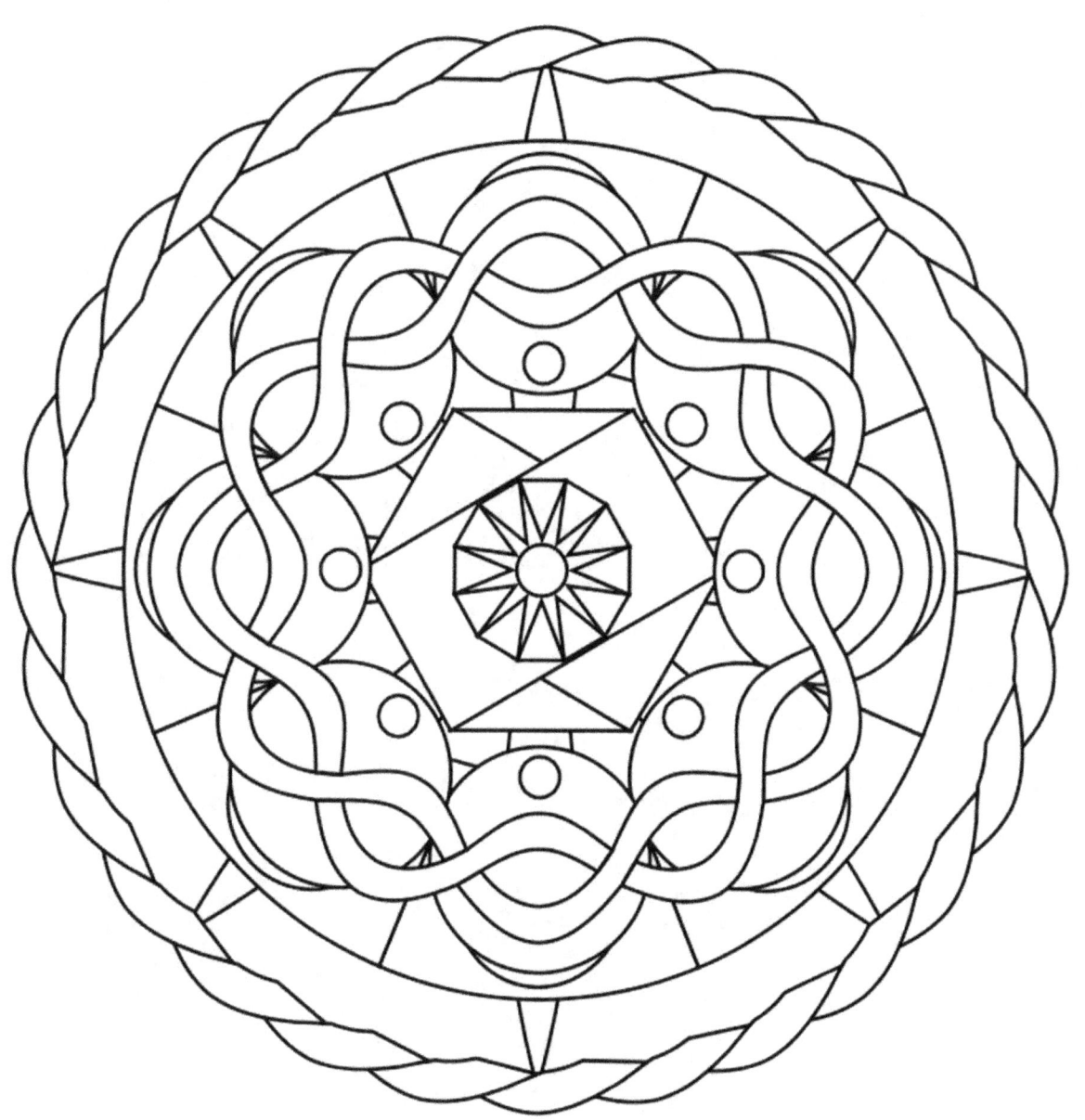

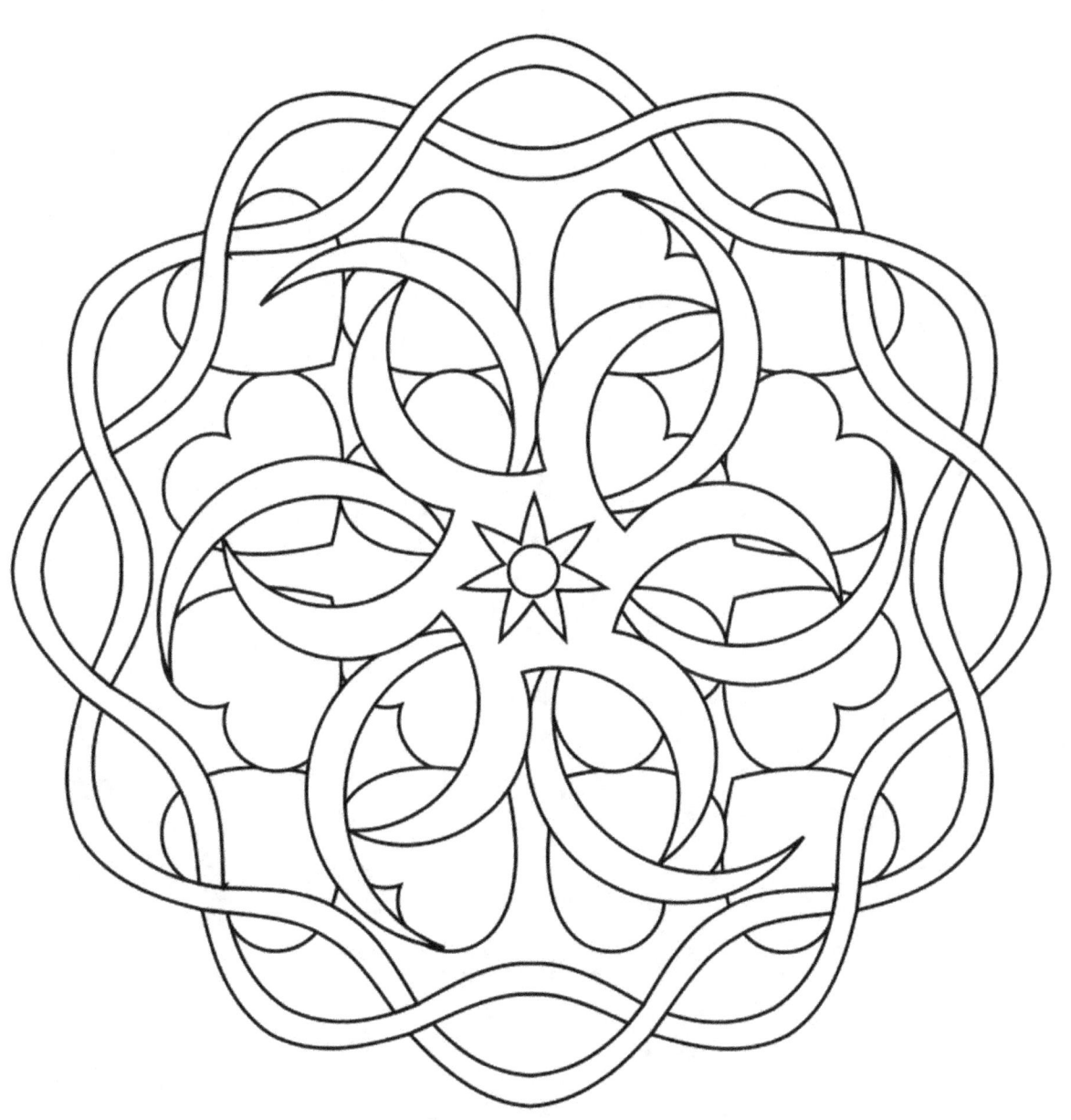

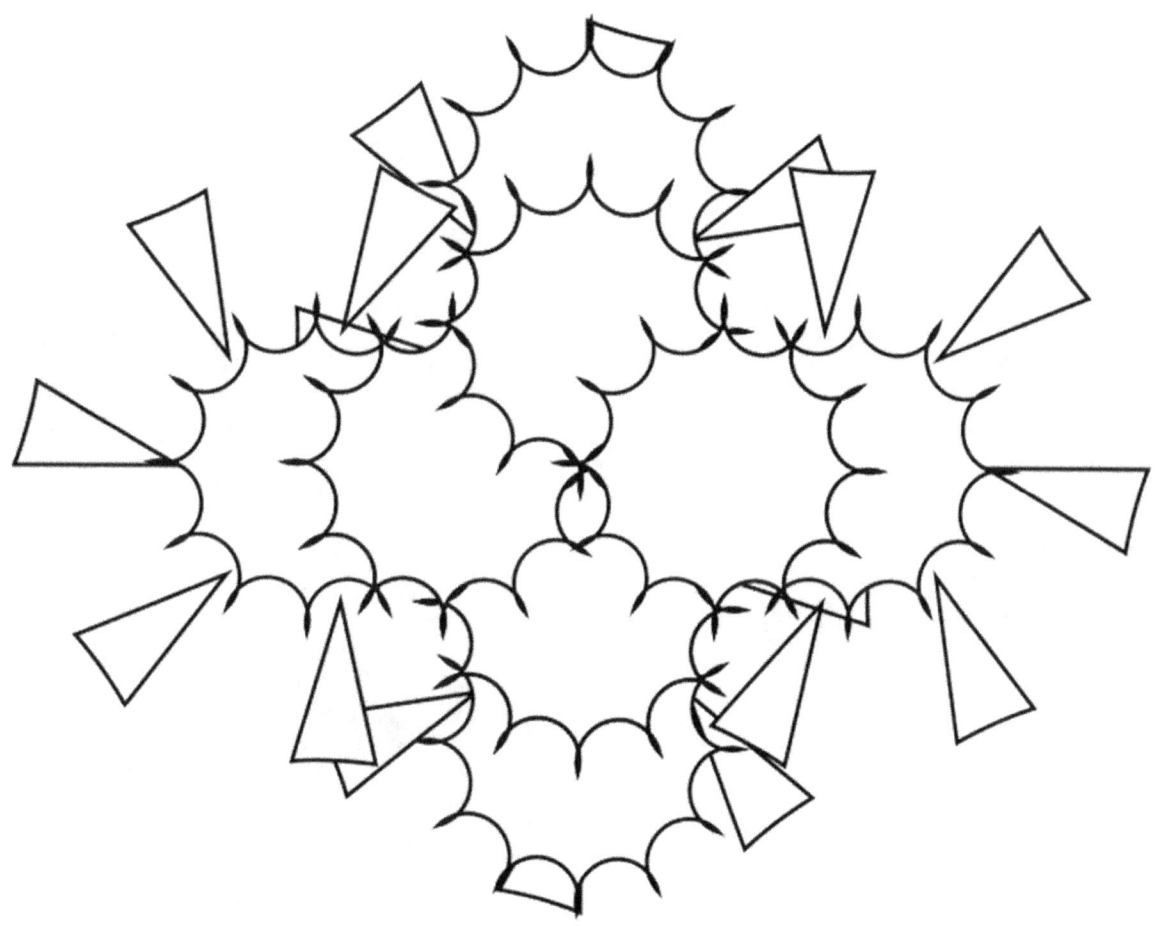

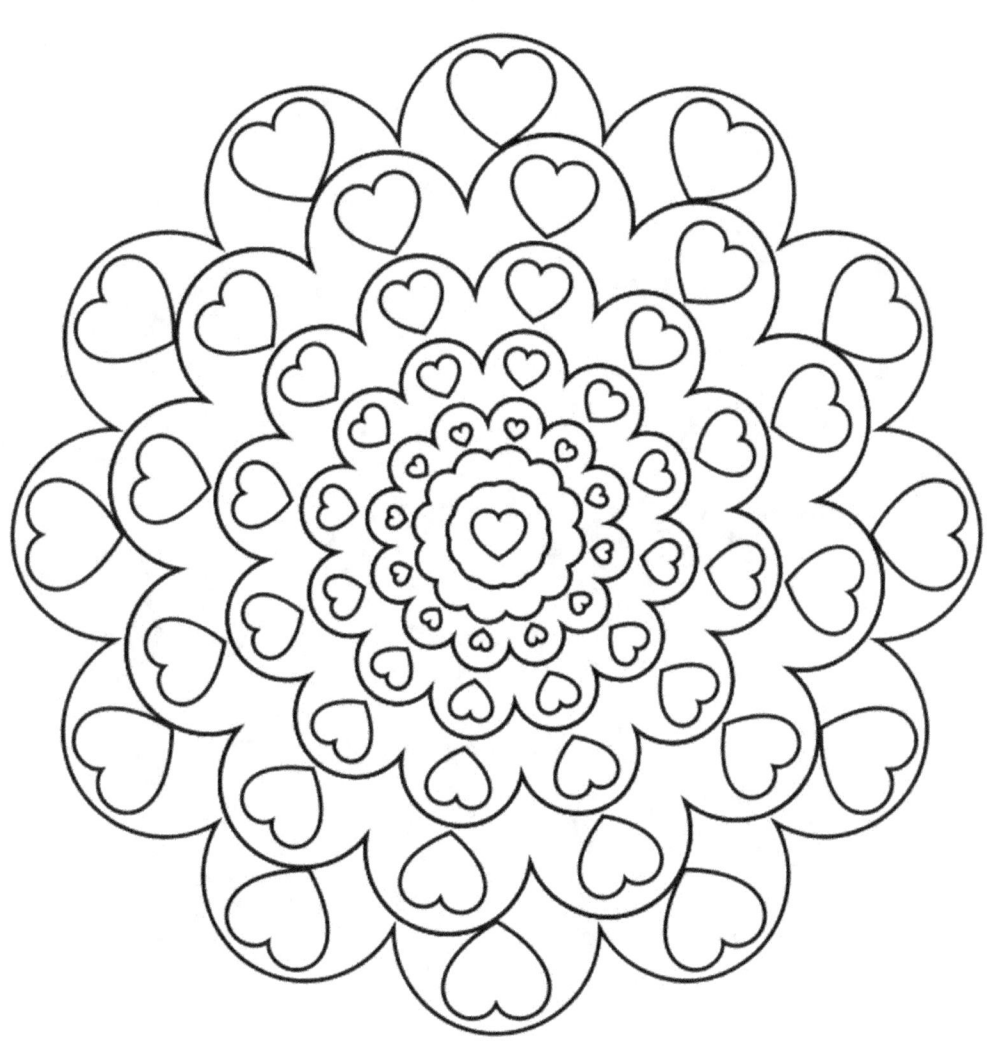

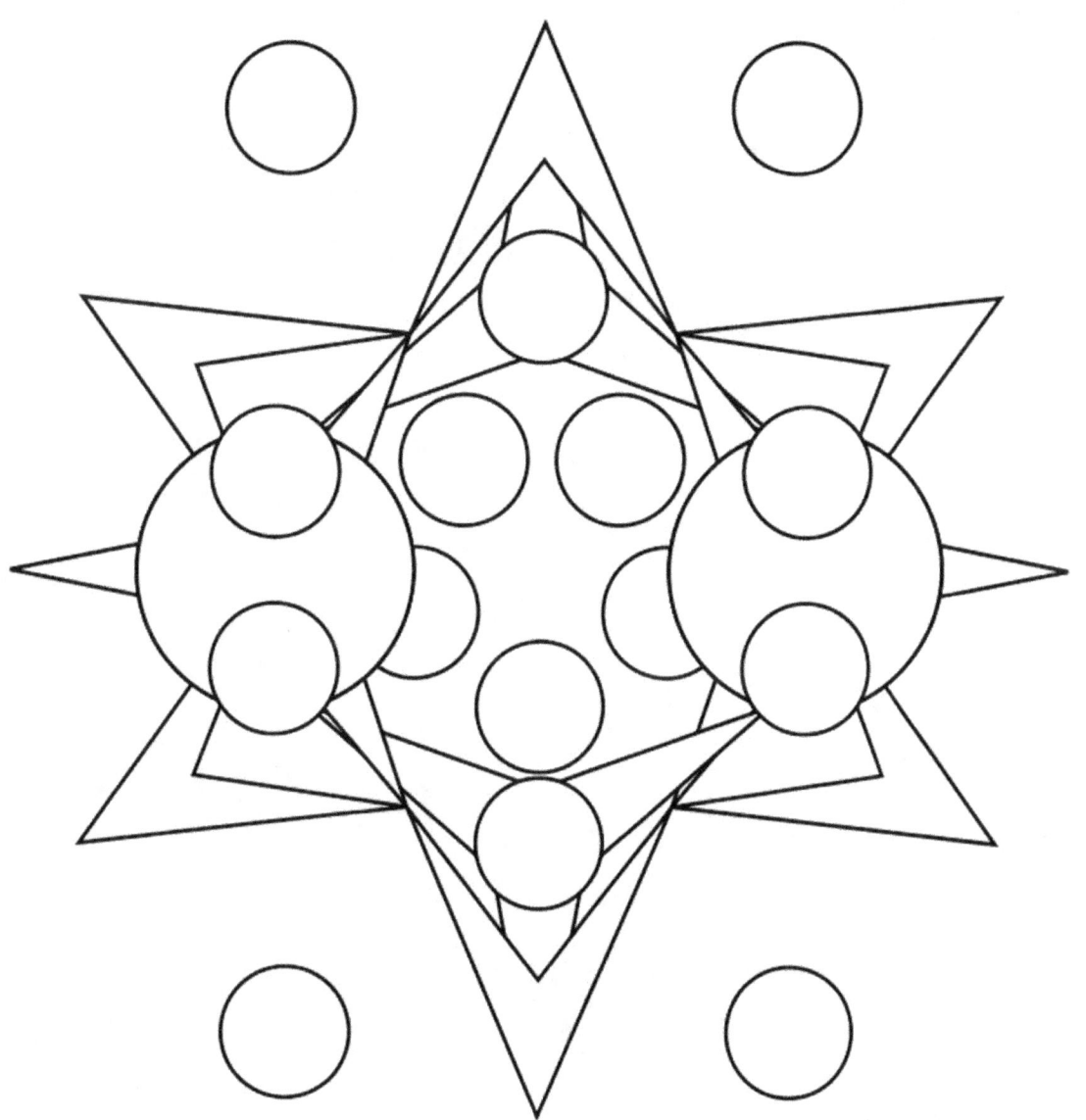

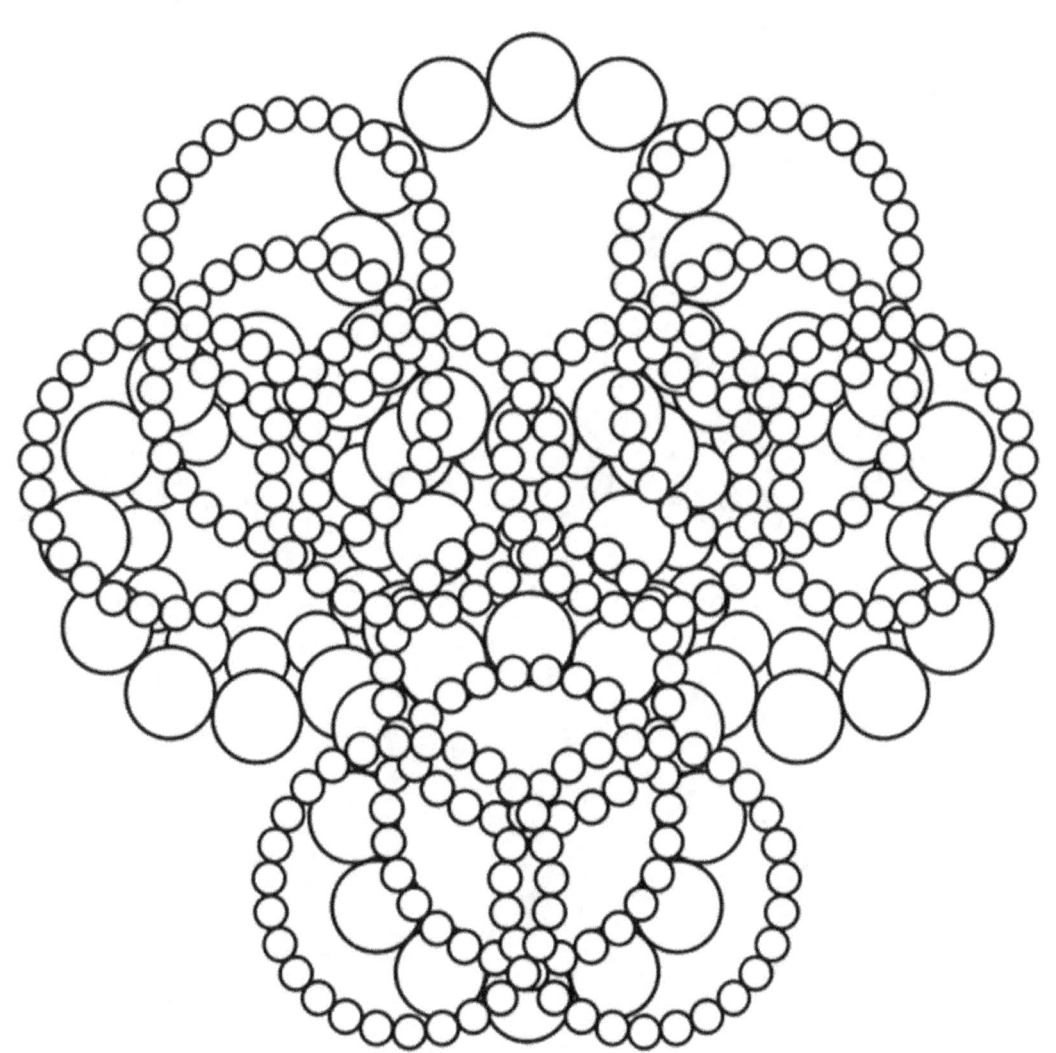

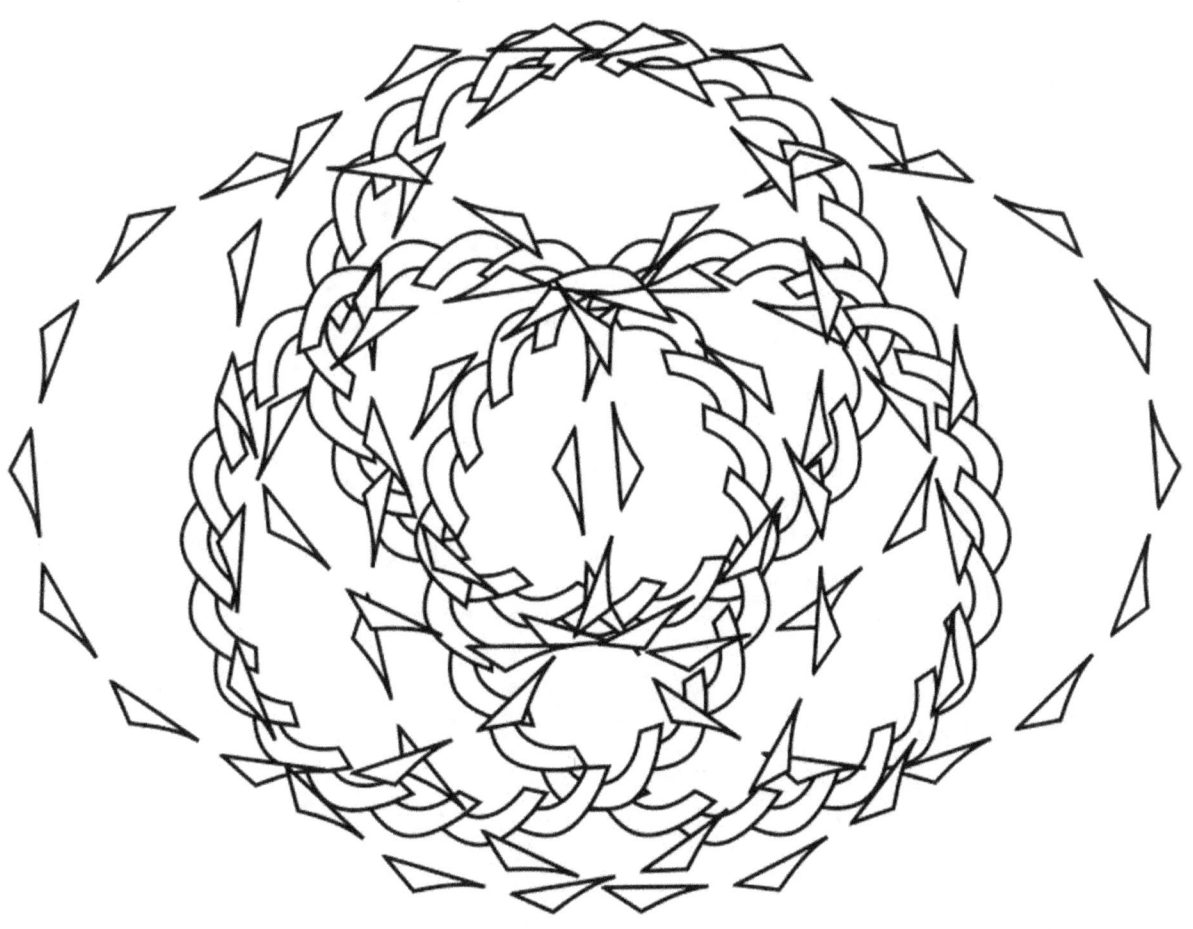

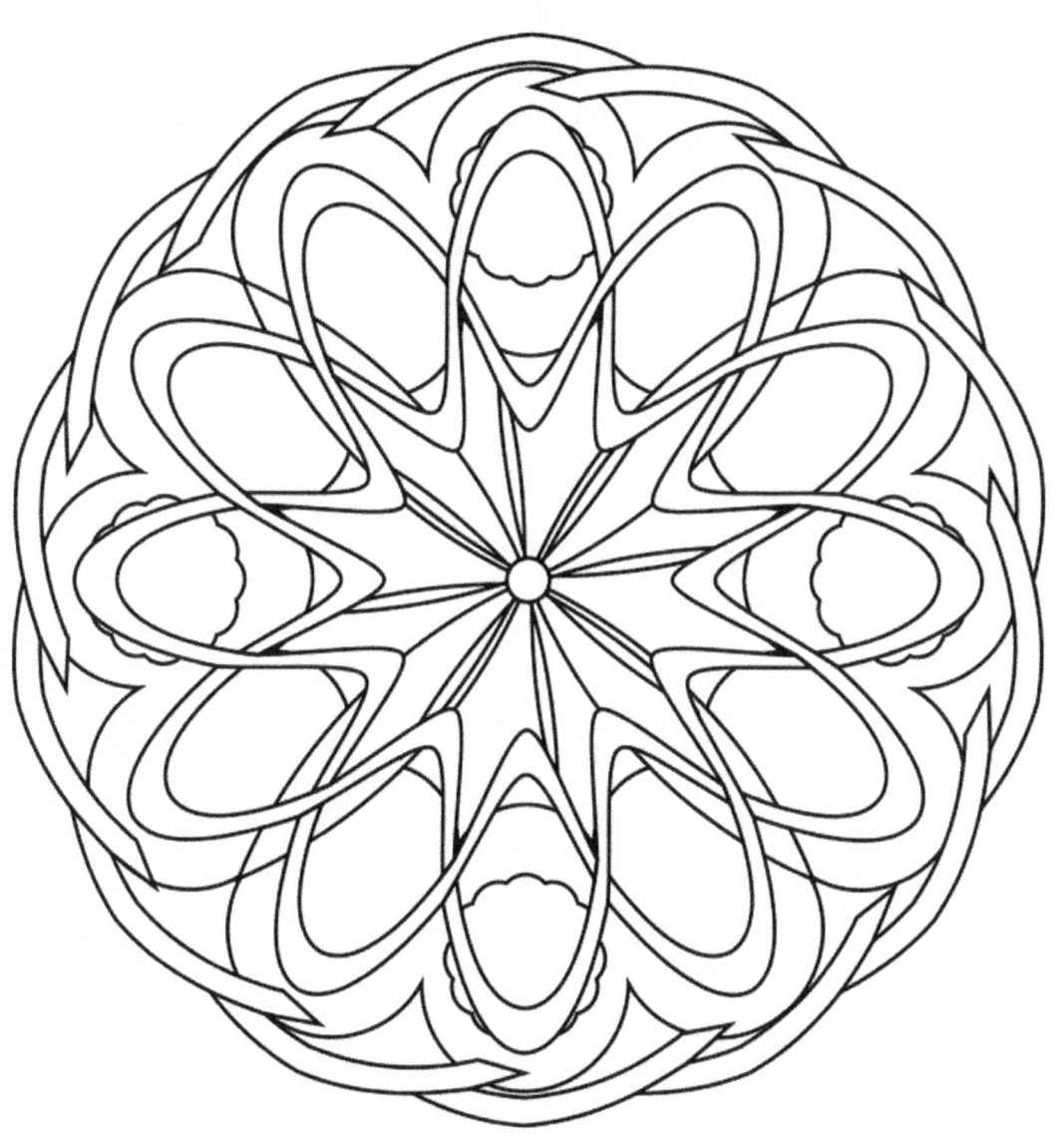

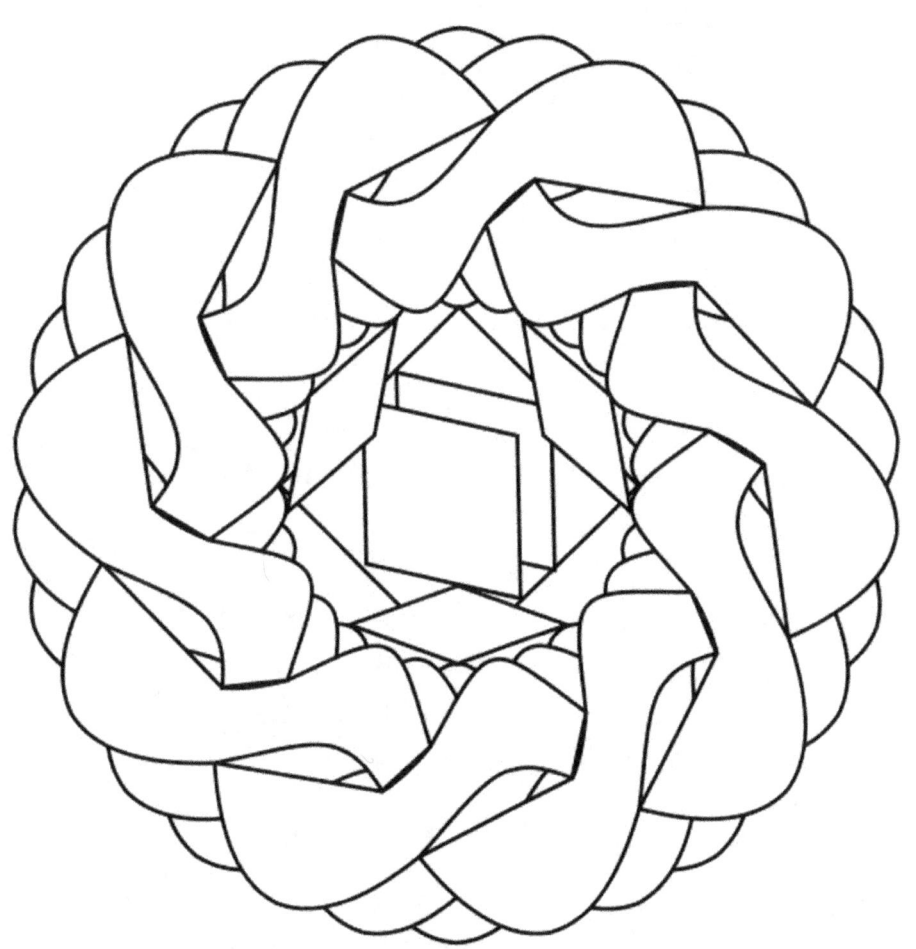

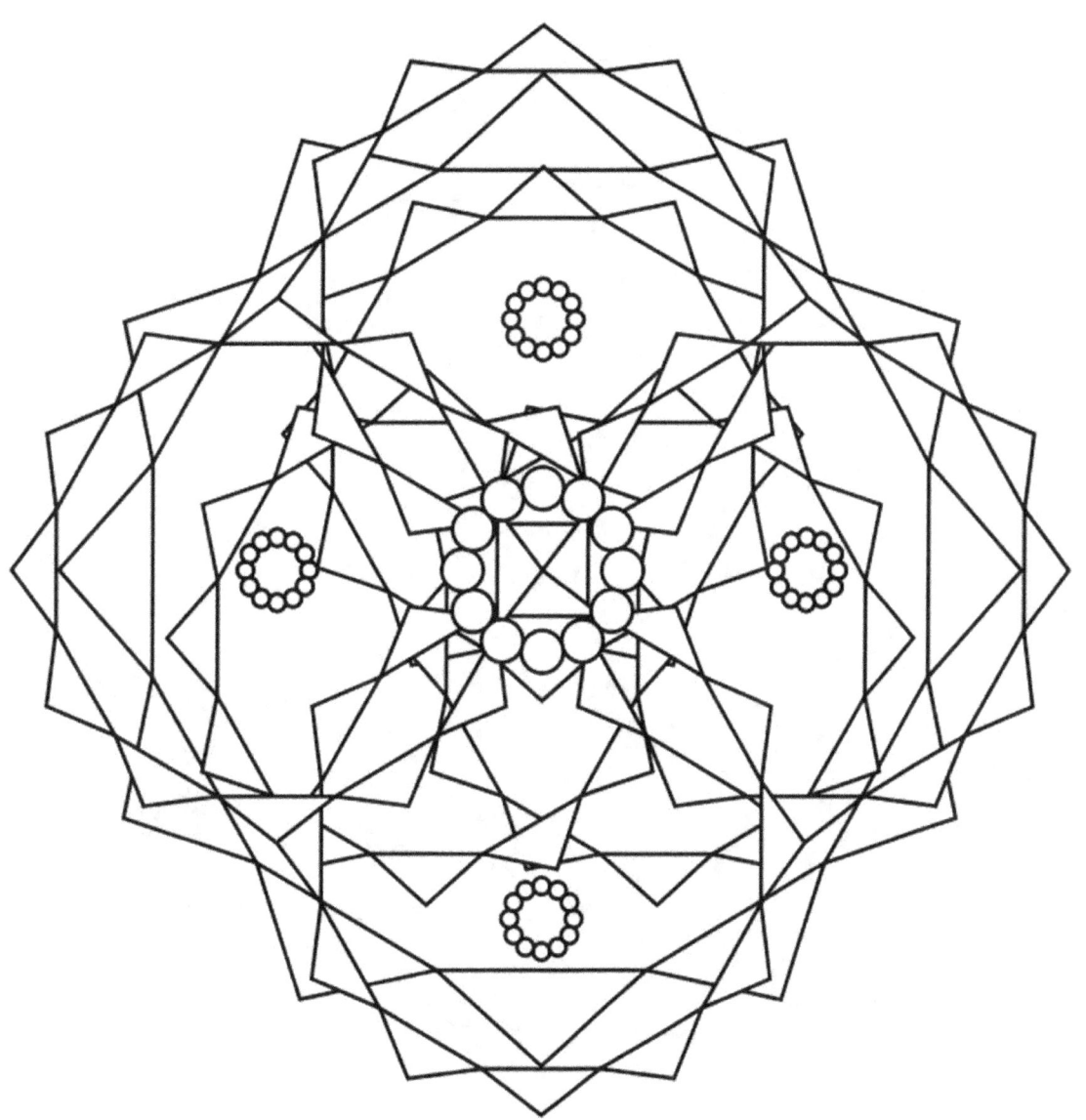

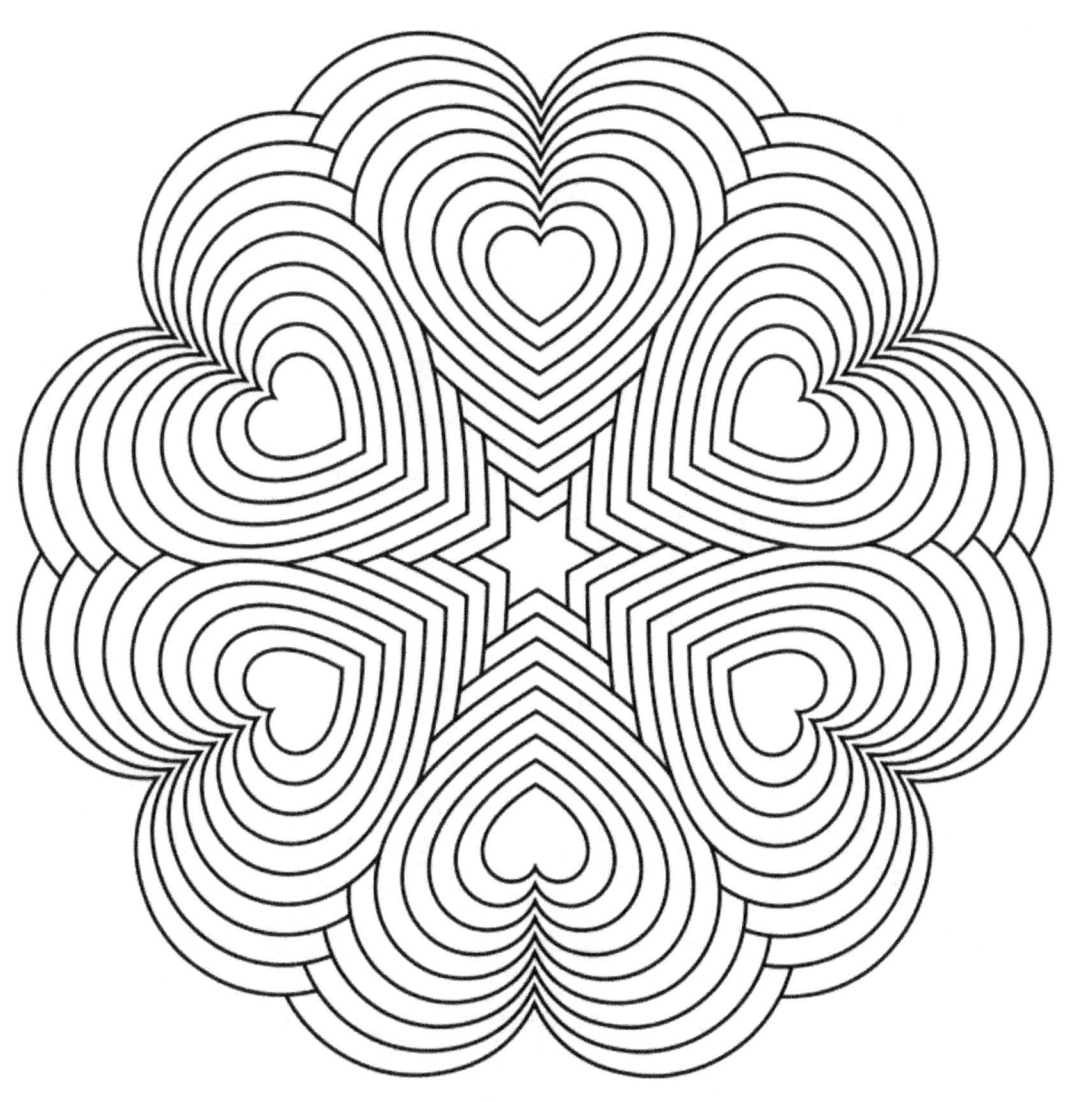

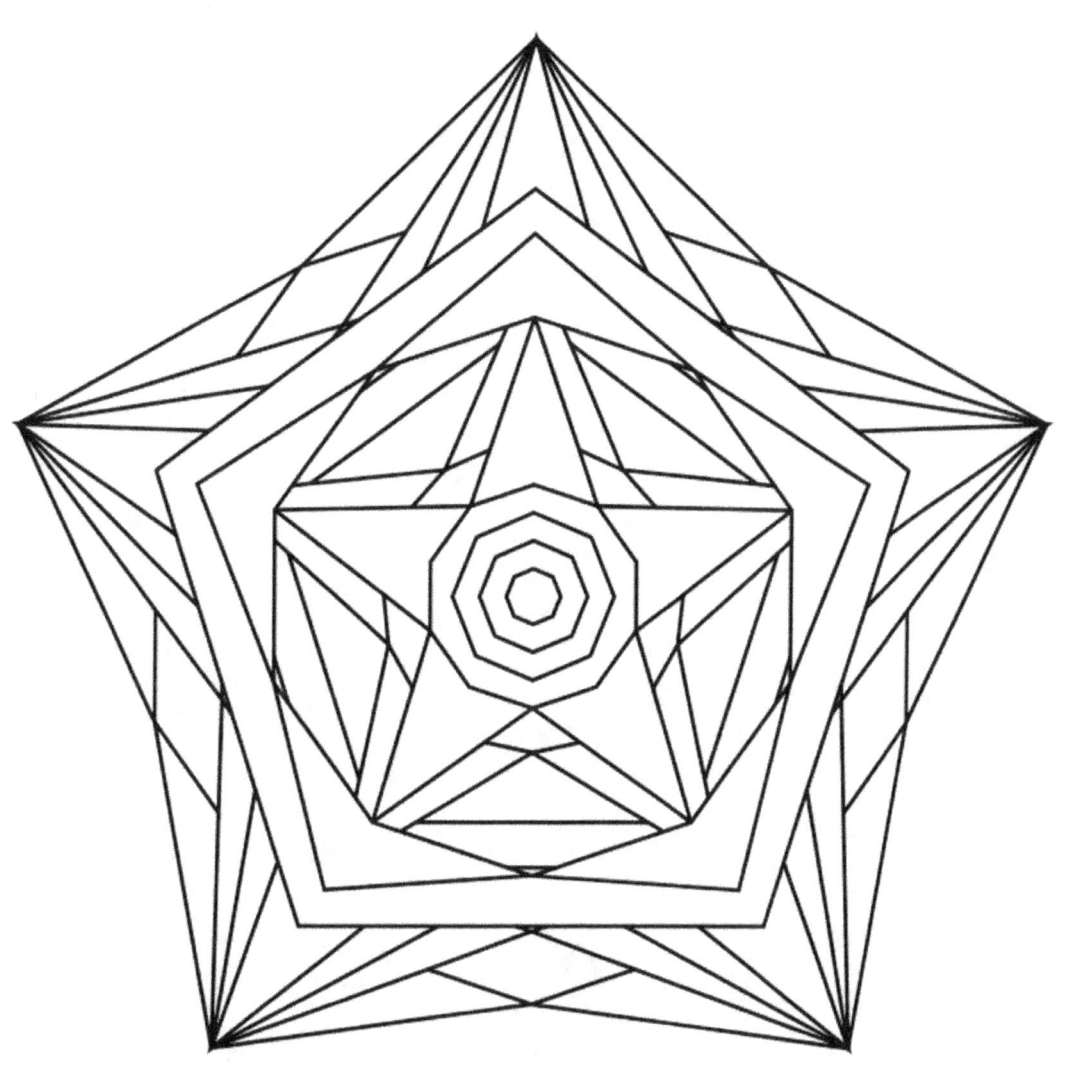

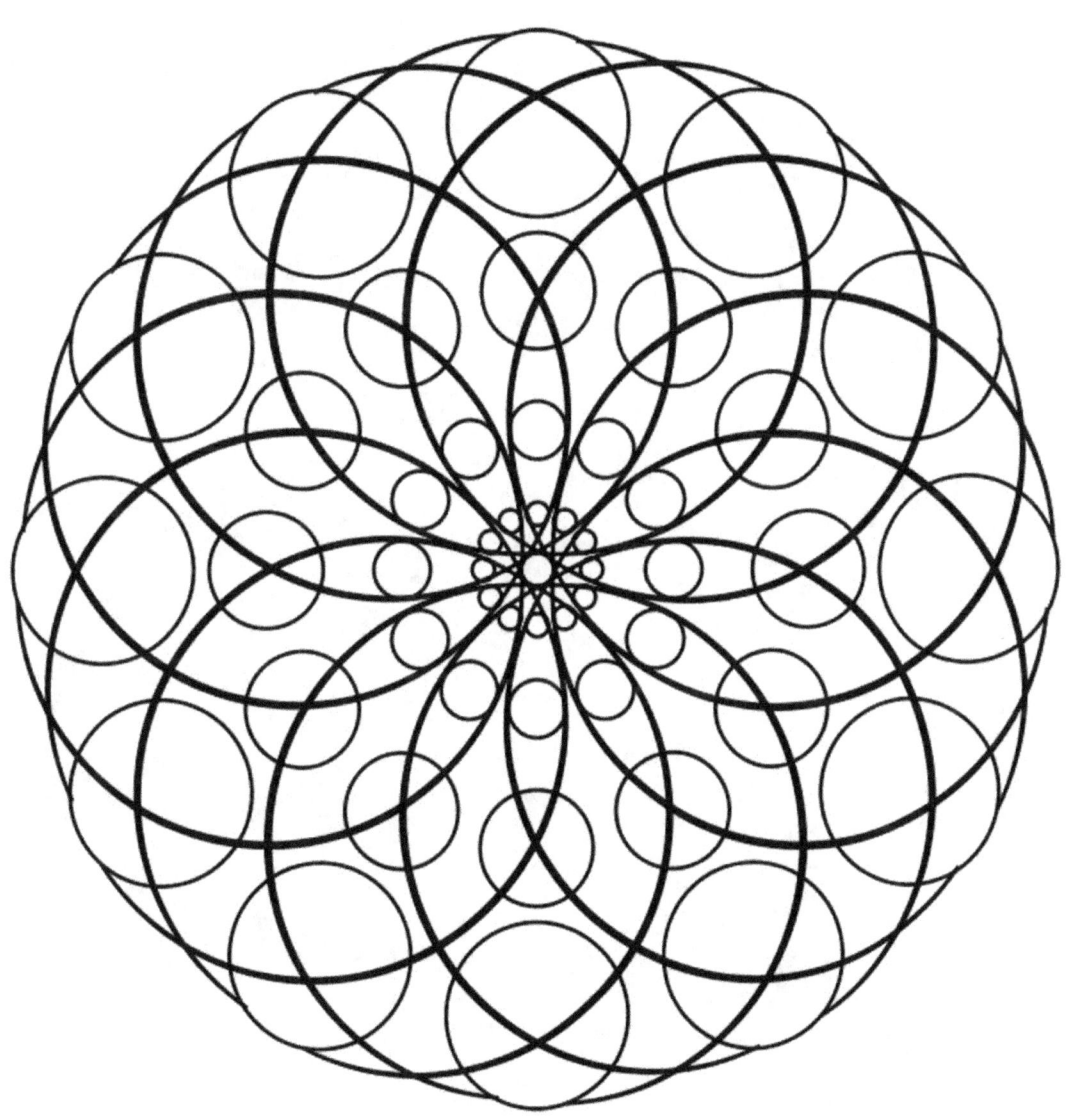

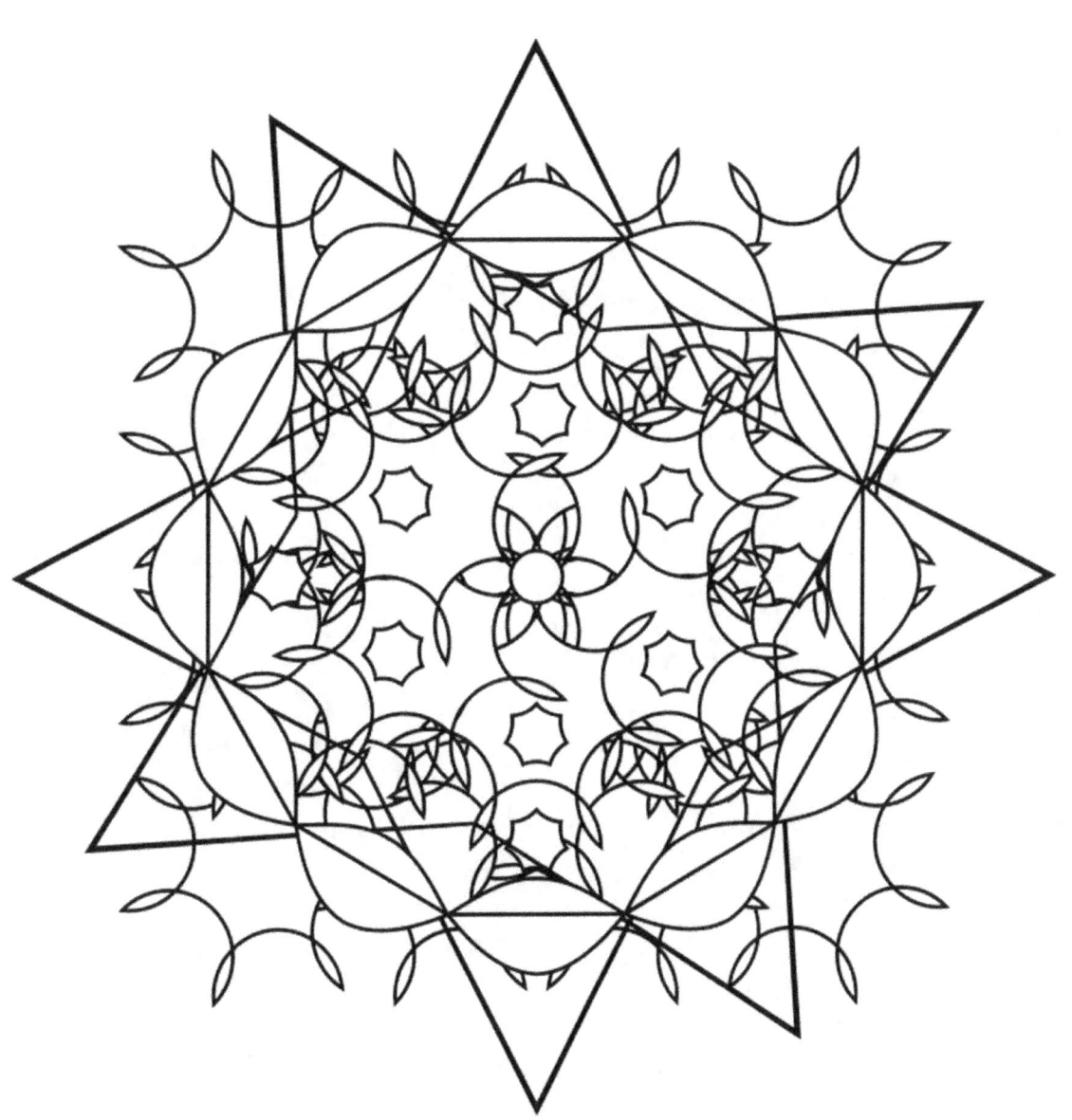

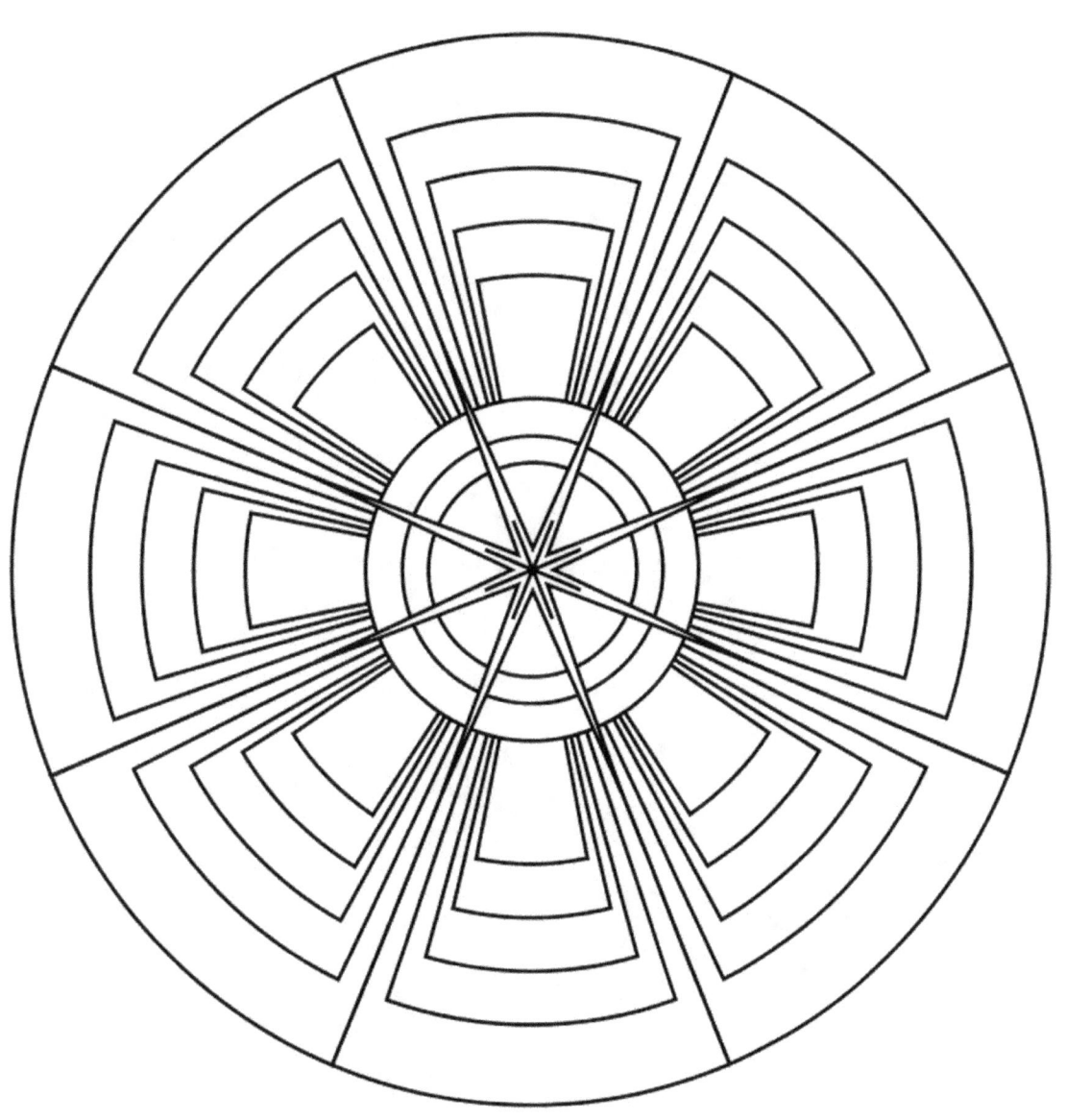

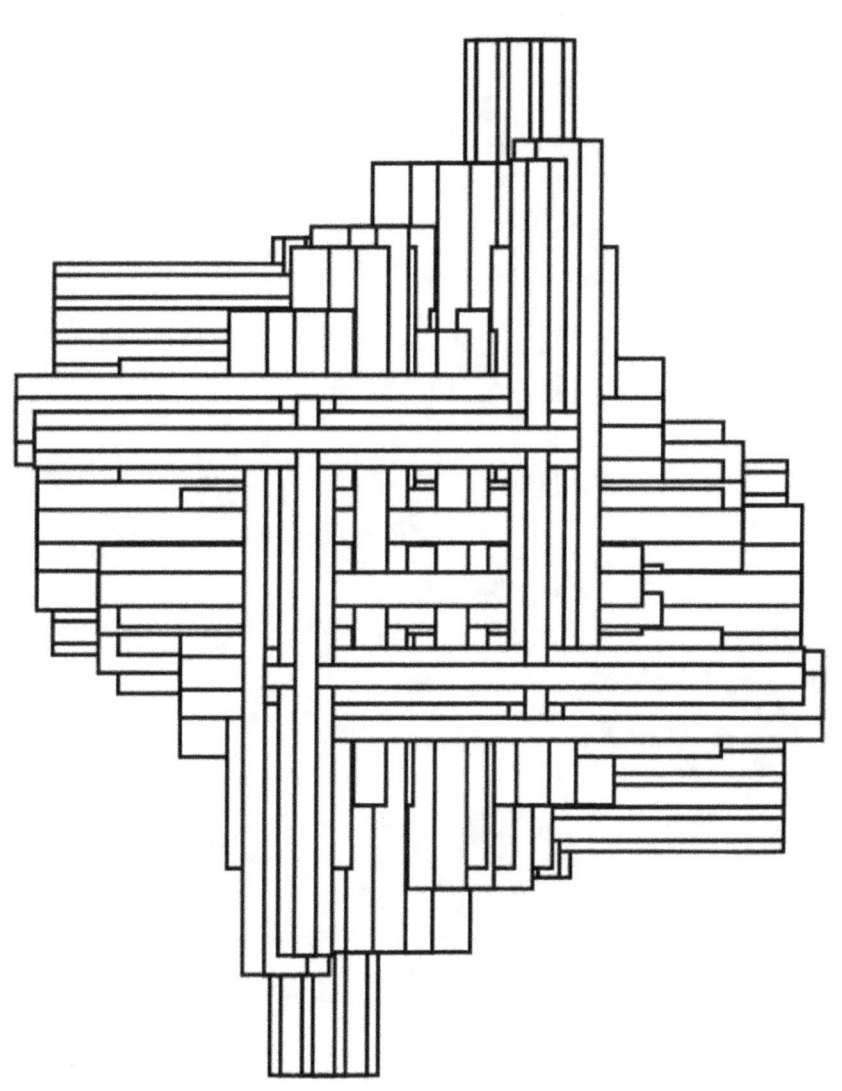

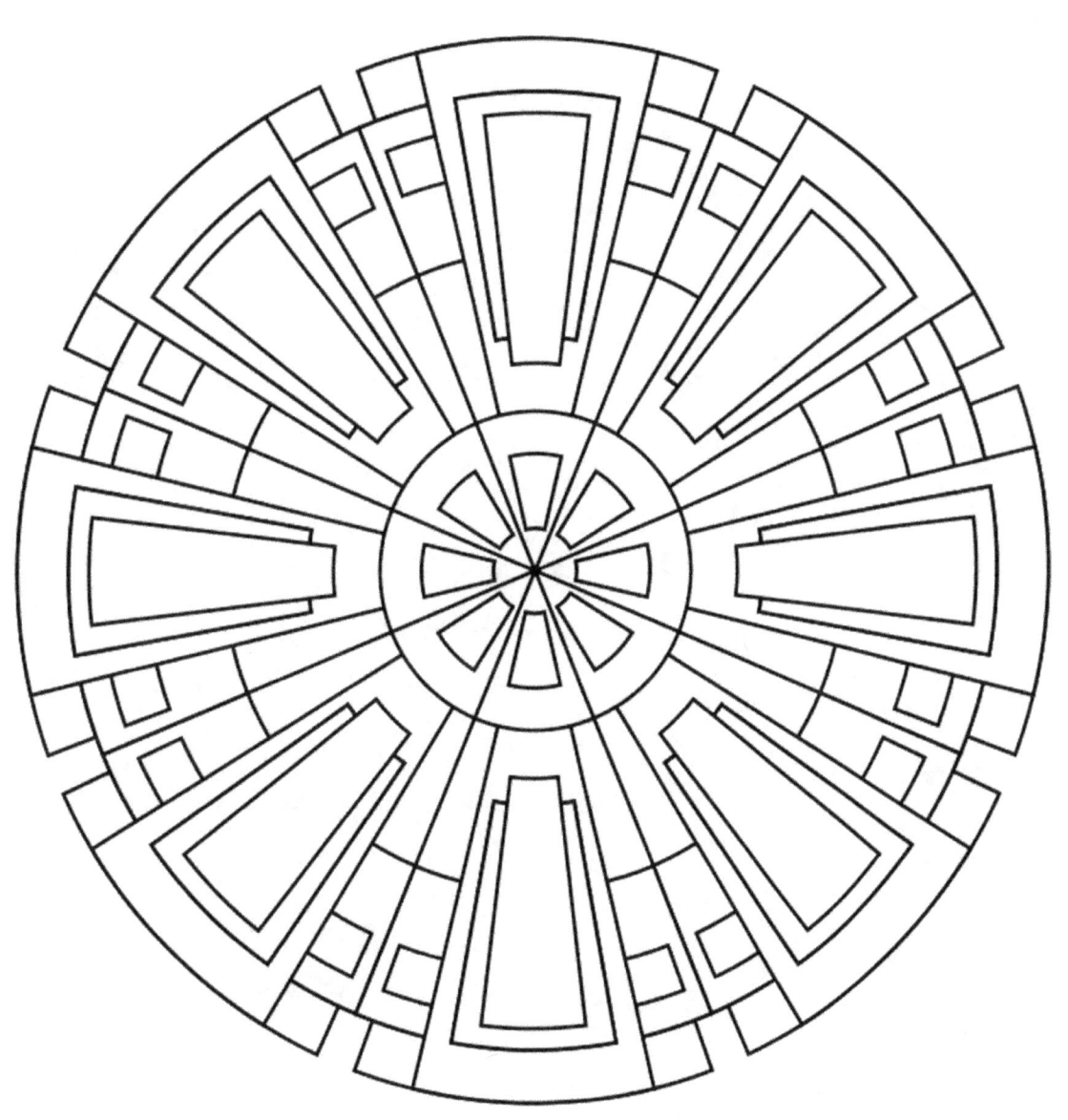

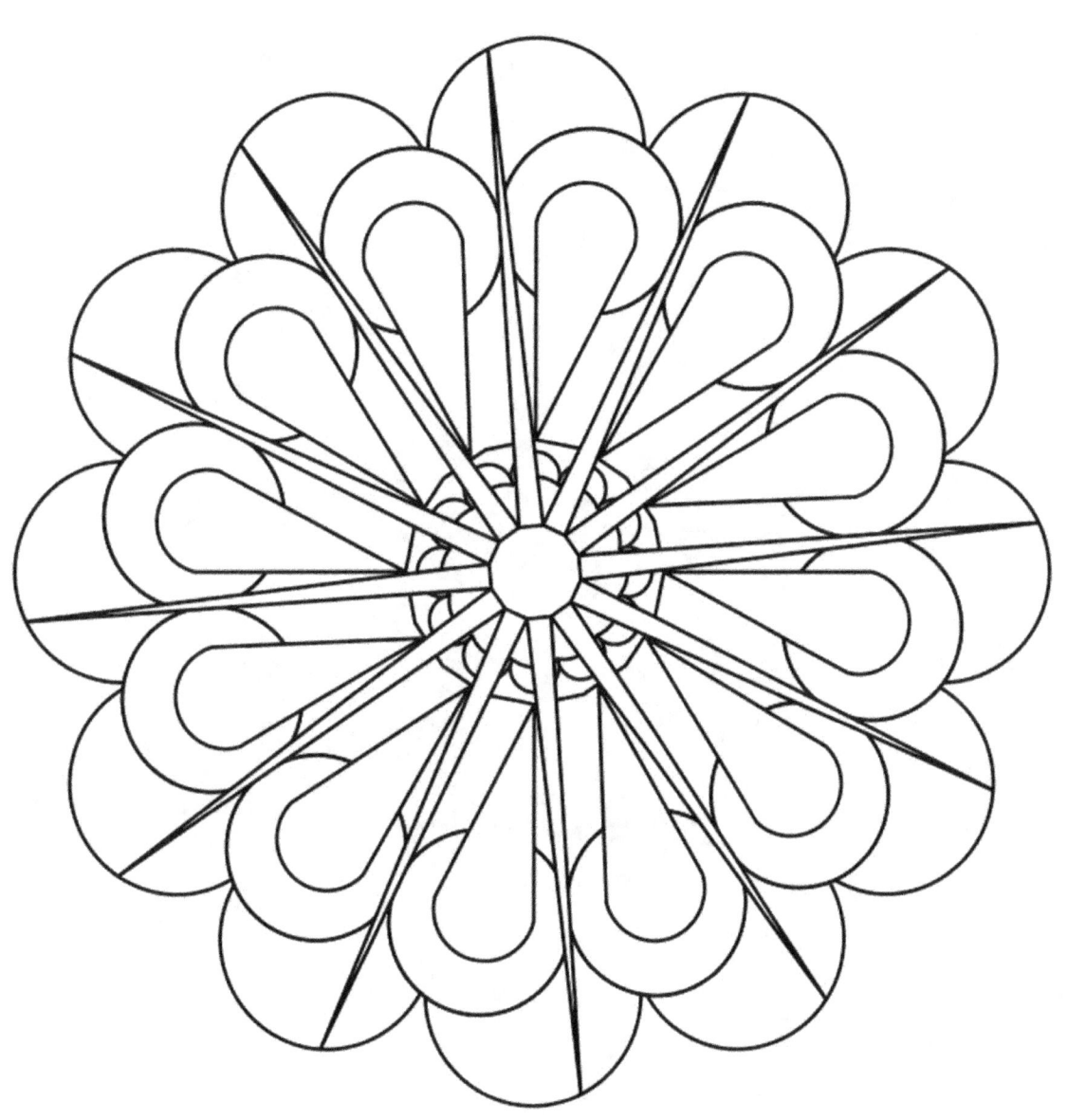

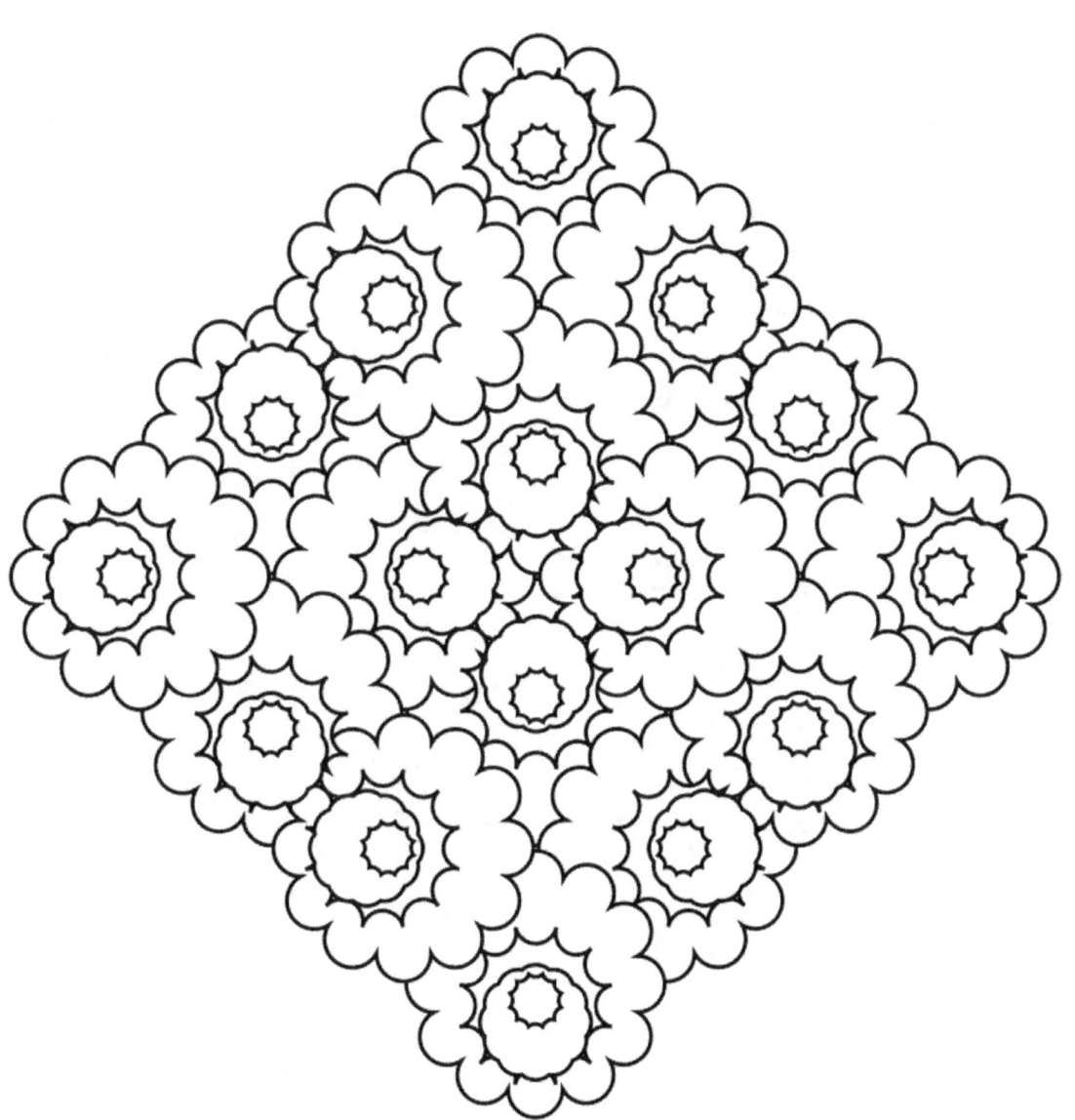

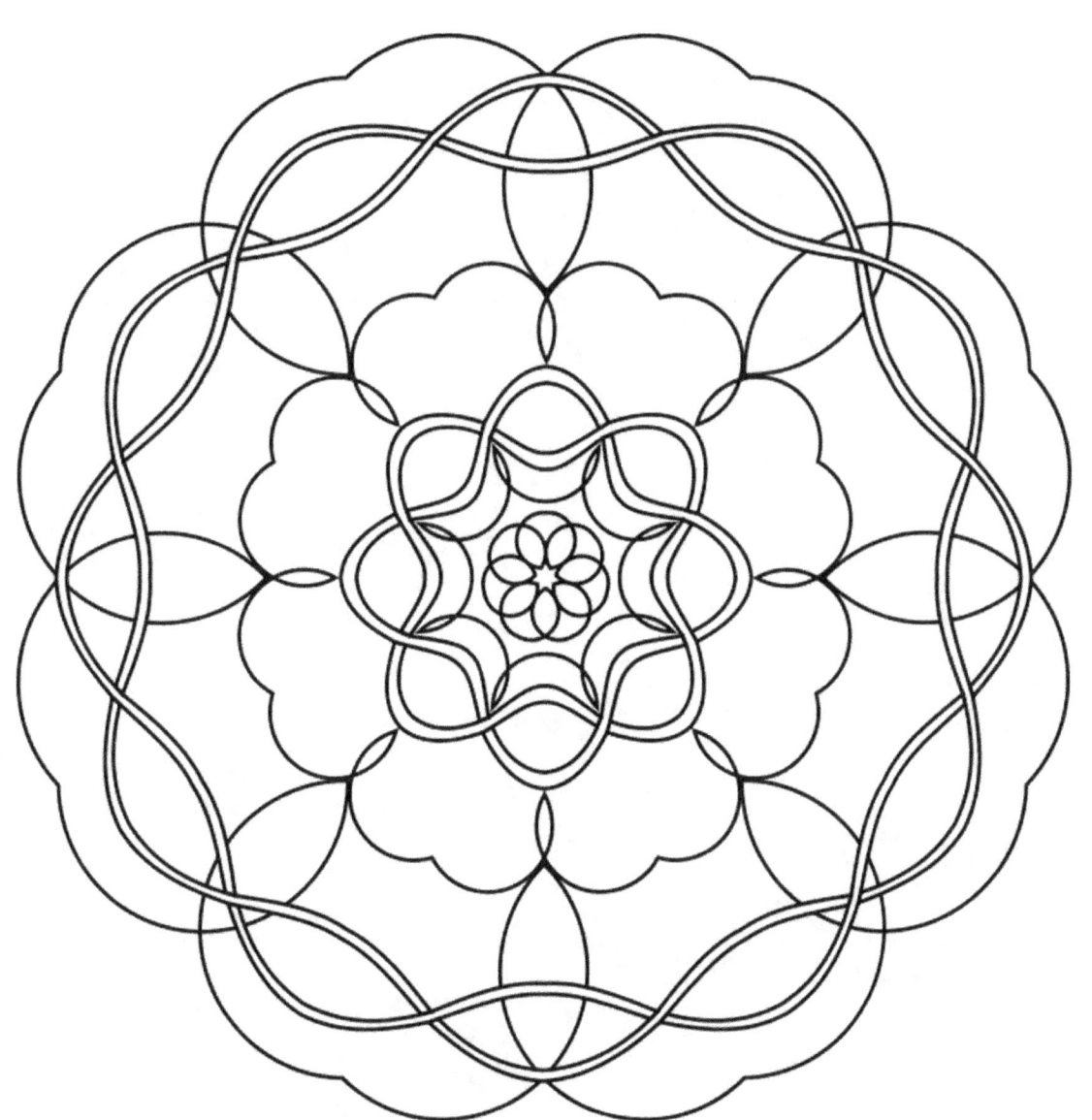

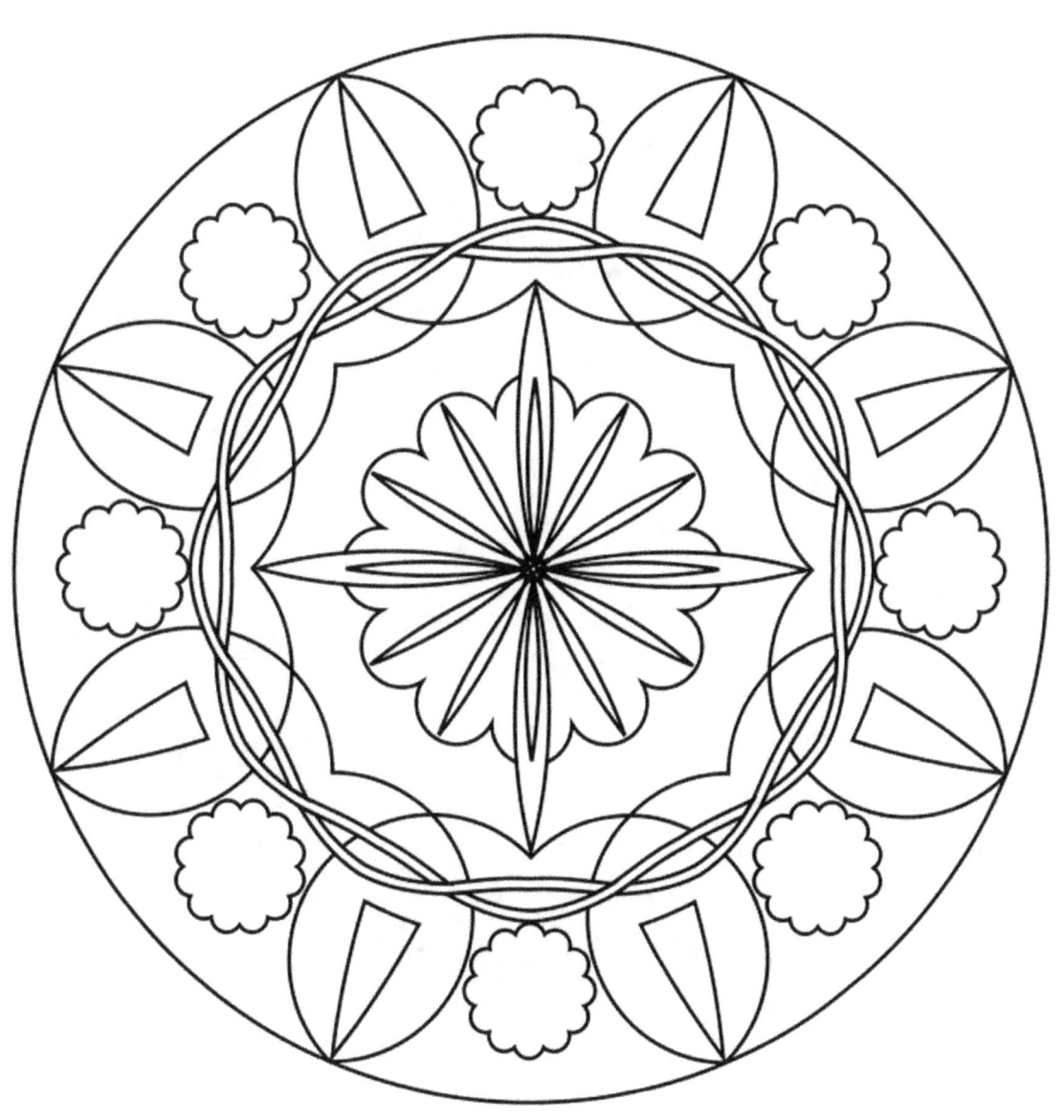

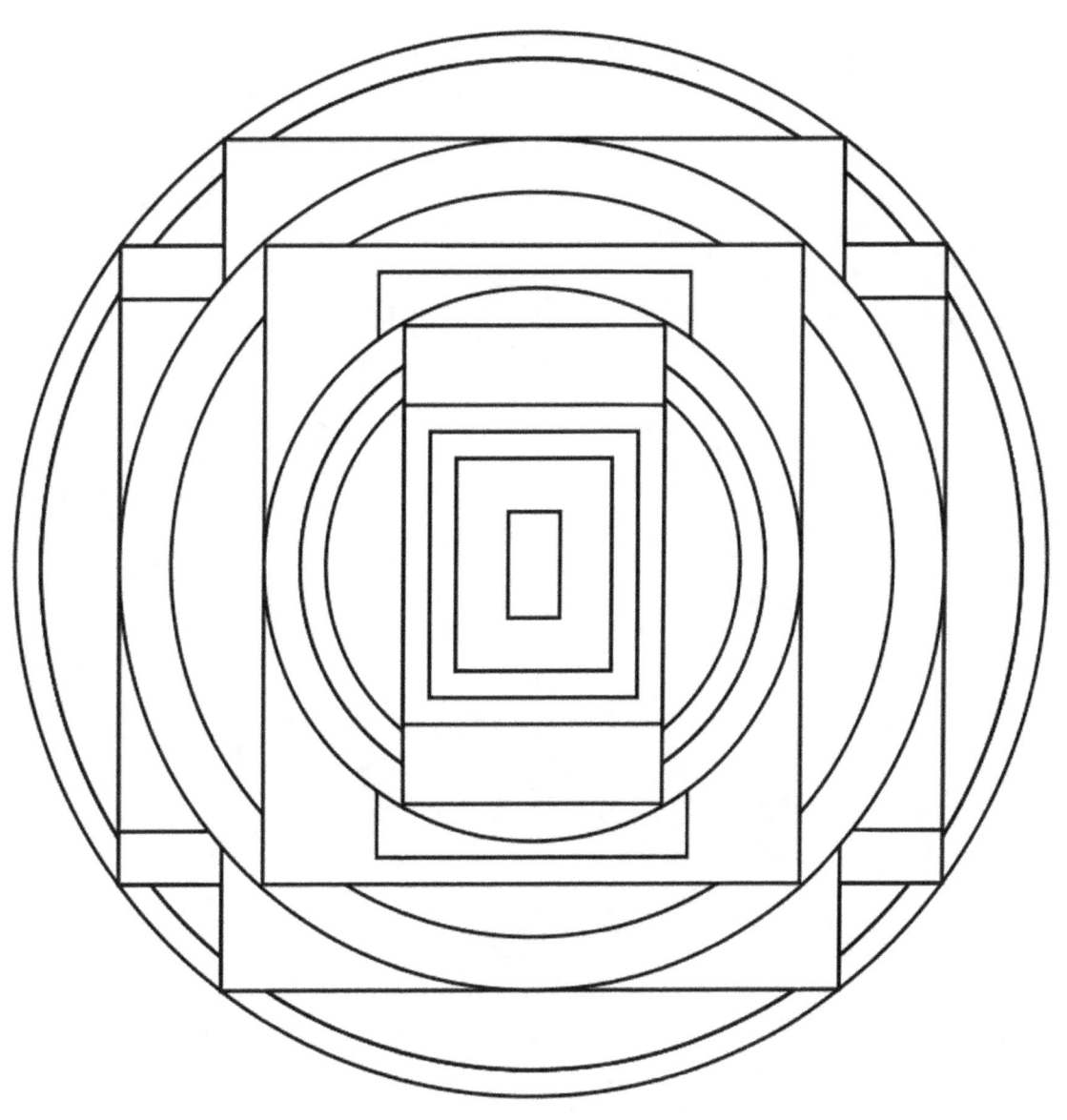

Thank you for purchasing and coloring this book.

You will find my other coloring books on Amazon.com by typing my name, Ruth Mason, in the search box.

If you enjoyed this book, please leave a review.

Email me anytime at favoritesofruthies@gmail.

www.ingramcontent.com/pod-product-compliance
Lightning Source LLC
Chambersburg PA
CBHW081605170526
45166CB00009B/2833